Wisdom Grows in My Garden

Rabbi Paul Plotkin

AIA PUBLISHING

Wisdom Grows in My Garden
Rabbi Paul Plotkin
Copyright © 2022
Published by AIA Publishing, Australia
ABN: 32736122056
http://www.aiapublishing.com

ISBN: 978-1-922329-44-8

This book is dedicated to my grandchildren:
Aryeh, Ellie, Akiva, Jonah, Sela, Nava, Liam.
They are my most special seedlings planted in the
Great Garden of Life.

Contents

Foreword

The first garden that most of us experience is the biblical Garden of Eden. Since the description of its planting follows the first chapter of Genesis, many people assume that this story is sequential to the creation story. First God creates the world, then He creates man and woman, and later He creates a garden for them to live in. It is a common thought and entirely untrue.

In fact, the garden story is part of a different narrative altogether. If the first chapter of Genesis is meant to teach us about creation of the universe and our world in particular, the second chapter that contains the Garden story teaches us about humanity. The story tells us that God created man from the dust of the earth. He then created this magnificent garden for him to "till and tend."

The garden is a physical place of fruit trees, vegetables, and animals of all kinds. Man is free to eat of all the fruit, but there is a special tree, the tree of knowledge of good and evil, and eating from that tree is a capital offense. There is knowledge in this new world, but it cannot be readily consumed. Rather it must be discovered, studied, digested, and acted on.

In Hebrew, earth is called *adama* and man is called *Adam*. From the very beginning, humans and the earth have been inescapably connected, and from that connection, lessons of life emerge.

The Garden teaches us about loneliness, and how we have a fundamental innate need for companionship and relationships.

We meet the snake and learn about temptation, deception, and pure evil.

In punishment and expulsion from the Garden, we learn about gender roles, and how they were established in antiquity. In the garden we confront mortality when, as a result of our actions, we are banished and told, "For dust you are, and to dust you shall return."

Life in the Garden was easy, but now humans discover how difficult the real world is and how much stress comes from living in it. Sustenance is no longer guaranteed, maternity and delivery will be painful, and nomadic wandering is the new norm. In expulsion we experienced fear and pain, anxiety, and stress. And we have been trying to cope with it ever since.

Some people find help in therapy, others in religion and prayer. Some meditate, and others focus on social justice to relieve the stress and loneliness of life.

I believe that returning to a garden is one of the ways nature allows us to reduce some of that stress, while at the same time teaching us about life.

In the excellent first season of the television show *Genius* (episode 10), Albert Einstein says, "Look into nature, then you will understand everything better."

It is the conceit of *Wisdom Grows in My Garden* that the garden has much to teach us about life and how better to live and manage it. To listen to its messages is to learn how to navigate through life. The garden has been a great resource for me in my life, and I hope sharing my experiences will help you find your way through life, using the lessons I have learned and continue to learn from my garden.

Chapter 1

The Love of Food

Ilove food. I love to gaze at it, inhale its aromas, experience its textures with touch and taste. I will boil it, fry it, grill it, and most importantly consume it. And like so many of us, it loves me back, as shown by my life's losing battle against an expanding girth.

It wasn't always that way.

Shortly after my second birthday, it was time for our family's annual migration from the heat of the city to the comfort of the cottage. This was our version of human transhumance, even if it was not a search for the metaphoric better grazing land—except, as it turned out, for that one year it may well have been.

Our cottage was owned and operated by my grandmother, a Polish Jewish immigrant to Canada who I lovingly called "Bubie." She arrived uneducated, of peasant stock, and engaged to my grandfather, who had apprenticed in Poland as a cobbler. She had dreams of marrying and raising a family in greater affluence than she could have ever seen in Poland, and with full religious freedom to practice as Jews. For her there was no greater sign of her success in North America than chubby children and even chubbier grandchildren, of whom I was then the first and only. That is where the problem started.

During the winter and spring that preceded that fateful summer, two biological events occurred that would shape the rest of my life: My mother became pregnant, and I was hospitalized for malnutrition.

Short of a Cossack uprising, I can't think of a greater affront to my grandmother than that in this land of plenty, her first born grandson—symbol of the future of her line, the depository of all her hopes and dreams—was hospitalized and for, of all things, malnutrition!

It wasn't that I was neglected or abused, God forbid. It was that I just wasn't interested in eating. I would spit out most of what was spooned into my mouth. The hospital eventually put enough calories into me so that I was fit to be sent home, but to my grandmother, the gauntlet had been cast.

At the same time, the other biological event, my mother's pregnancy, would come to play a major role in my grandmother's response and ultimately to my relationship with food.

My mother was due in early August, and when the time came to pack up and get ready for the summer escape, the doctor would not permit her to go. It was too far away and too isolated to even think of going into labor, what with no car and no phone save the phone booth in the village. So that summer my mother was "grounded."

My mother and father were trapped in the city, but not my grandmother and her new ward. We would now spend the summer in the healthy atmosphere of the country, unfettered, unchecked, and under the total dictatorial control and power of Bubie on a mission.

Based on one's perspective, it would become the summer of

rectification or the summer of revenge. But one thing was clear: I was directly in her crosshairs, and the blight of malnutrition was going to be obliterated from this world, and maybe into the world to come.

Not since the invention of foie gras and the forced feeding of the poor goose has there been such an onslaught of fattening up one of God's creatures. Day and night, she fed me. I have no recollection of the details—I was only two years old, after all—but I heard about it twenty-four years later in a surprising and embarrassing way.

I was a newly ordained rabbi "enjoying" my first pulpit in Vancouver, Canada. Friday night services were always followed by a social hour called an *oneg* where congregants would mingle, enjoy some pastry, tea or soda, (pronounced pop for the rest of us) and of course come up to the rabbi with some comment about the sermon or my favorite approach.

"Rabbi, if you have a minute, I have a question I've always wanted to ask . . ."

I was new to the congregation, so having a stranger come up to me at the oneg was by no means rare, but the course that this conversation would take was entirely unexpected.

"Rabbi Plotkin, are you by any chance the Paul whose family had a cottage on Cameron Avenue in Jackson's Point, Ontario?"

My heart started to race. Someone here in the city I had just settled in, and where I knew no one, not only knew me but knew my favorite place in the whole world. A place located on the other side of Canada! How exciting!

But who was he, and why did he not look even a little familiar?

"Yes, I am he, but who are you?" I asked. "How do you know me?"

"I'm Doctor Freddie B. We had the cottage diagonally across the street from you. I am older than you, and we sold the cottage when you were still a child, so you won't remember me."

I didn't remember him, but I did remember the family name, and then he said it. I can still remember my reaction: looking for a place to hide and hoping no one had heard the conversation.

"Your Bubie used to chase you up and down the street with a bowl of soup, or a glass of milk, a kaiser roll, or just about anything she could get you to eat, all the while yelling in Yiddish at the top of her lungs, '*Pinchesell, ess a bissel!*'" (Paul, eat a little!)

I don't know if it was the content of what he said or just hearing my Hebrew name pronounced as a Yiddish diminutive that embarrassed me more. Having a Hebrew name that is pronounced *Pin-Ch-As* and sounds like a pain in the a— was curse enough growing up, but hearing it in this context was even worse. He was giving eyewitness testimony to the summer of Bubie's revenge.

That scene must have played out all through July. I can only imagine from later years what the menu was like. Calories did not exist, since that was a foreign term to my Bubie. Greasy fat was good, and covering carbohydrates with it was even better. Every unhealthy specialty of the Jewish Eastern European diet was proudly prepared and then doggedly forced upon me. *Schmaltz, potatonik*, onion buns, roast chicken, fried potatoes, *p'tcha*, and her version of *kishka*, followed by homemade blueberry buns, *mandel* bread and something delicious she called *shtichlicht* (my mouth is watering as I write this).

July turned into August, and the onslaught remained even as my resistance declined and then evaporated. I was no longer an adversary. I was now a willing coconspirator. She no longer had to chase; I was standing by the pot waiting for a taste, a lick, or a bite.

On August 9th my sister was born. There was great joy throughout the family. Transportation had to be arranged so Bubie and I could be taken to Toronto. She would see her granddaughter and I would meet my sister.

In those days mothers would stay in the hospital for at least a week, so I was taken up to my mother's room to see her. It was the first time in about six weeks. Bubie brought me in, and my mom warmly greeted her and then asked who the little boy was that she brought with her. When Bubie (proudly, I imagine) reacquainted her with her son, my mother started to scream hysterically, "What have you done to my son? Where is *Pinchas*? This is not the slender boy I left you with! What have you done?"

Bubie's work was now complete.

Now you understand why I love food.

Next came my love of gardening.

Chapter 2

The Miracle of Growing

For many years, decades actually, I returned from Florida to the cottage in the summer. Even when I lived for two years in Vancouver and had two babies, I would fly back for a month to enjoy the cottage, the lake, and the family. I was a third-generation cottager, my kids were the fourth generation, and we all have our own wonderful memories.

We had a neighbor who came up for the weekends who had a wonderful hobby. He grew vegetables in his garden on his property. He would come up every year in May, during Ontario's long weekend, and plant the garden.

By the time I got there, I would see the growth that had emerged or was submerged. There were different kinds of lettuce, scallions, potatoes, rhubarb, peas, and so much more.

I would watch him come up on Friday afternoon, tend his garden, and then select what was ready to be harvested and turned into dinner for that night. I always thought how wonderful it was to grow, harvest, and cook something that you had started from seed.

I noticed others who had larger plots and raised significant quantities of zucchinis, tomatoes, cabbages, and more. There was a famous lakefront inn in town that offered golf and delicious food. The chef was blessed with an enormous garden, raising a variety of vegetables and herbs, and had a wonderful raspberry patch. I could just imagine the delectable desserts he was concocting. I was jealous. I was like the kid looking through the knothole in the fence, wishing I could be doing what they were doing. But I couldn't.

Our property did not have enough free land to grow anything of significance, and I was there for only a month. I could never get anything into the ground in time to be there for the harvest. I discussed my frustration with my neighbor, and he suggested I try to grow some raspberries. They came up by themselves in the spring and were ready to be harvested in July, when I would be there.

There was a fence between our cottage and the next that received ample sunlight, and I could plant on my side. It seemed all too easy to me, but literally what did I know?

New raspberry plants were always growing out from the older growth, and so another neighbor dug up a few for me, and I planted them near the fence. Then I left for my home in Florida.

A year went by with no word about those little plants, and I had no expectations. They had spent much of the year under a lot of snow, so could they really have survived?

In late June we flew to Toronto, got into a family car, and drove to the cottage. The visual biorhythm of the drive was intact as always. The cornfields had their endless rows of one-foot growth running off into the horizon. The yellow color of the fields of rapeseed reminded me of the fields of sunflowers in Tuscany. The milk cows wandering aimlessly around the barns elicited calls from the kids of "Look! Animals!"

The same sights I had seen every late June from the back seat, as my father drove his car in what seemed like an endless trip, were now visible to my kids in the back seat on a trip that seemed endless to them.

The only difference this time was the hope, faint as it might be, that maybe one of the plants had survived. Maybe there would be a berry or two this summer, even as I knew deep down there would be nothing but grass near the fence, waiting for me to mow it all down.

We made the turn off the highway, down the one mile stretch to Main Street, looking for signs of change in the area and knowing there wouldn't be any. Left at Main Street, straight for four blocks and then the final turn into the street where our cottage was.

We passed the same majestic trees, the same empty lot, the same dwellings, and the same parking spot in front of our cottage. And then I spotted it. Something near the fence that had never been there.

I jumped out of the car and ran over to see it. I stood in total disbelief. A patch of canes had grown up in an area that had always been grass, surrounded by leafy plants and, wonder of wonders, the canes had blossoms on them, and some even had the beginnings of recognizable berries.

To me, I had participated in a miracle of biblical proportions. I had created something new. I had nurtured a living entity and I would get to eat fresh raspberries.

I was hooked.

Chapter 3

It is Always Harder Than You Thought

For the next few summers, I tended an ever-growing patch of berries. I learned its life cycle, I learned to cut down old canes to make way for next year's new ones that would hold the raspberries, and I encountered pests.

It seemed that after the first year, nature decided that the "freebies" were over, and now I would experience the dark side of growing. At first I didn't know what was going on. I could see areas that should have been the beginning of berries but were being destroyed instead. I didn't know what, why, or how, but I perceived a real threat to my crop. I hadn't waited and dreamed for a year only to come back and not get any berries. I had to get a closer look and figure it out.

As I got on my knees and edged up closer to the bush, I noticed white foam on different parts of the canes. I had no idea what it could be, but I grabbed it between my thumb and forefinger and realized it wasn't just foam. Something solid was giving resistance to my touch. I blew away the foam and held onto the solid and then saw it in all its ugliness. A little grub had been born inside the cocoon of foam, with the express purpose of moving its way up to the berries and eating my crop. (As you will soon see, this is a theme I return to repeatedly.)

This will not do, I thought, though I'm pretty sure I thought it in language that would not be appropriate for most social settings. It was the genesis of the dynamic of me versus them, which would only grow in intensity and violence in the years to come.

I had an immediate flash to a short story I had read in junior high school called "Leiningen Versus the Ants." It was later made into a mediocre film with Charlton Heston, titled *The Naked Jungle*. He was a plantation owner whose vast estate was threatened by a plague of ants. In my scenario I was Leiningen, and the grubs were coming to take over my "plantation."

Now that I had discovered the problem, the solution seemed obvious: Get some pesticide and kill the grubs. Except for one problem: I was determined to grow organically. What could I do?

That is when I discovered how to organically deal with little pests. Find them, squeeze them, and move on.

I now knew that growing raspberries was going to be a little harder, take more time, and demand continual vigilance. That was the first lesson I learned from gardening:

1. Nothing worth doing is going to be easy, especially if it started that way, and even with hard work, the results would never be guaranteed.

This lesson became invaluable to me as a rabbi, especially when called upon to deliver a eulogy. I would often make the analogy of farming to parenting. Both the farmer and the parent clear the field, plant the seed, raise and nurture the seedling, and watch it grow into maturity with great anticipation of the harvest and no guarantee of ever enjoying one.

We can do everything in our power to see to the success of the little ones and still not enjoy the fruits of our labor. We use the best fertilizer, we feed them the healthiest of foods. We remove the weeds and plant supportive vegetation nearby, we send the kids to the best schools, and we encourage them to find the best friends. We do all we can and not always perfectly, yet under the same circumstances, one plant thrives and another dies. One child achieves success, and another spends a life in failure. Such randomness exists because in both plants and children there are not only external elements but also the internal DNA that has its own plans.

How many families do we all know where all the siblings were raised in the same household with the same parents and the same opportunities, and yet each one grew up differently?

Some parents harvest a full crop, others a partial one, and some get none.

With both vegetable-growing and child-raising, we must first acknowledge our limitations, and while we can pray for the best, we must prepare for a lot less. Life can be very humbling for gardeners, and perhaps even more so for parents.

Chapter 4

Man Does Not Live on

Berries Alone

Raspberries were fine but in the end, they were just berries. I longed to grow a tomato, gather pounds of zucchini, and maybe even grow a red cabbage. I dreamed of a dinner menu in which all but the protein came from my garden. But how? Where? I only had a month.

I vented to my hero, my neighbor, about my frustration, and he answered me with a question that shockingly had never entered my mind.

"Paul, you live in Florida. Why don't you garden there? In fact, your growing season is twice as long as ours."

Why indeed?

Sometimes you become so fixed in your thinking that even the obvious becomes invisible. Summer is for growing gardens, and winter is for the land to lay fallow. Country is for growing and nature, city is for work and indoor activities. It never crossed my mind that since South Florida raised much of the fruits and vegetables for the United States during the winter, I too could grow vegetables at home.

It was time to get out of my comfort zone and try something radically new: Plant a garden in my backyard in Margate, Florida, a bedroom suburb of Fort Lauderdale.

Chapter 5

All Beginnings Are Difficult

In Rabbinic literature we find the statement, "All beginnings are difficult." It was easy in Canada, where I was a visitor and not a resident, to plant the berry patch. It was low effort, high reward and truly a novel hobby to help fill open vacation time. But home was serious. Home was work. Home was an eleven-hundred-family congregation who all looked to me as their personal rabbi, and I was.

In pre-computer and pre-cell phone days—and yes, there were pre-computer and pre-cell phone days—I could spend two hours a day just returning phone calls. If I was going to plant a garden, then I was making a commitment to myself that I was going to carve out time from an impossibly busy day to dedicate to the needs of the garden. Was it a reasonable expectation? Probably not, but my mother had raised me with a statement only time would prove true and insightful: "If you want to get something done, give it to a busy person."

I went to the library and the bookstores, called the county extension services for their publications, and read all I could find on backyard gardening in South Florida. Let me emphasize *South* Florida, because the differences in southern, central, and northern Florida are significant.

Some things are universal. Vegetables needed consistent watering, a certain PH in the soil, and no less than six hours of full sun a day.

South Florida is blessed with great weather but awful soil. Because of the wet season and the copious rain we receive, the soil has evolved in a way that lets the water drain quickly. This is great for the soil, but awful for the plants. Nutrients wash out quickly and easily before the roots have a chance to fully absorb what they need. Therefore, my garden would have to have its soil improved with the addition of a lot of organic material.

The next decision was where to plant the garden. Unlike the cottage in Ontario, in Florida I was blessed with a lot of land. Even after the placement of the pool, there were multiple places to choose from to build the garden. Since soil was all bad and therefore irrelevant to the choice, and after determining that flat land would be preferable to a berm in the back, the next issue was the distance to the spigot. It had to be less than the length of available hoses.

I was now down to one variable: sunlight. That is when I learned my next lesson:

2. Think long term, even when acting in the short term.

It was August in South Florida when I began the reconnaissance in the backyard to find the perfect spot. I went out in the early morning to see where the sun first shone on the ground. I went out in the afternoon to see where the sun had moved to, and then later in the afternoon to see which area still had sun. *I'm so smart*, I thought, flattering myself. So smart in fact I knew better than to imagine the sun might not always be in that same August spot.

I was like the young executive that Annette Simmons tells of [1]:

> *His first job was drawing electrical engineering plans for a boat company. The plans had to be perfect because a mistake found after the fiberglass was formed could cost a million dollars. He was very smart. By twenty-five he already had two master's degrees, and he thought and acted like this job was beneath him.*
>
> *He received a call one morning from a six-dollar-an-hour worker who wanted to know if the plans were correct.*
>
> *He was incensed by the question. A few minutes later, the supervisor called with a similar question and received a snarky rebuke. It was only when the president of the company called him that he went down to the office and, while staring at the plans, he became more and more queasy. It seems that, being left-handed, he had transposed starboard and port, making a perfectly wrong mirror image of what was needed. The six-dollar-an-hour worker had saved his day and his job, and even more importantly, had taught him a lesson in humility.*

Similarly, I too was smugly sure of myself as I went through the

---

1 "The Six Stories You Need to Know How to Tell" Chapter 1. Annette Simmons

very tedious and painful job of removing ten by twenty feet of deeply rooted St. Augustine grass to prepare for the planting of the garden. Next came the hauling of the bags of topsoil, manure, and organic material. By late September I was planting my first seeds and seedlings, and I was full of optimism, until my arrogance was rewarded with the thunderbolt of reality.

The sun not only changes its location in the garden during the day, but it also changes even more dramatically during the year. The sunrise in September happens in a very different place than in November. The length of sunshine in the beginning of summer in South Florida is three hours longer than in the beginning of winter. If you put the garden in the wrong area, you will not get anywhere near the six hours that are needed. In that first year, I did not know this, and my plants reflected the loss. Some had a diminished yield, others yielded plants that were puny and underdeveloped.

Had I realized how much I didn't know, I would have asked someone with experience to look at my plans. Instead, I was so sure of myself that I eventually had to start all over in a new location.

Beware of self-assurance and smugness. Just when you think you know it all, you discover how limited your capacity for seeing everything really is. Don't be afraid to ask for help when making long-term plans, even as you act in the short term.

Chapter 6

If You Want to Know Yourself, Just Listen.

Several years later I was starting to get comfortable with the garden. I opened a second location which I knew would receive less than ideal sunshine, but I wasn't about to fill in the pool and its deck. I also knew that I could plant herbs in the shadier section and experiment with new crops in the sunnier parts. Rosemary, arugula, Italian parsley, basil, and oregano would give me what I needed for the year, even if I didn't set a record for herbs per square foot. Zucchini, on the other hand, resisted cultivation no matter where I planted it. Later in the book, I will share lessons learned through years of the "zucchini struggles," but for now zucchini played a different role. It opened a window into my deepest self.

I know one of the challenges we face in our modern world is a problem with sleep. Few of us get enough of it, and that affects our health and disposition. I know this is what my friend calls "first world problems," but when they tell you that inadequate sleep can lead to weight gain, you have my complete attention.

I finally figured out why I gain weight. It's not because of how much I eat or how little I exercise. It is how much sleep I'm not getting.

Sleep matters for rejuvenation, for healing, and for developing patience, but it also matters because sleep is when the brain does all its work processing the events of the day.

I have learned from Kabbalah, the ancient Jewish mystical wisdom, that sleep is when our higher souls leave the body and go into the non-temporal spiritual world. There they gather information and return it to the body, where we process the information in dreams. This is the best explanation I have ever heard to understand people who have precognitive dreams, about things that will and do happen later.

For those less inclined to see dreams in a spiritual context, just rely on the science of psychology and say that dreams are part of the processing of our subconscious. While we sleep, we are working out the issues deep inside us that we are struggling with, and which we may not even be aware of.

Too often we have dreams we know we experienced but cannot recall any of the details. Some therapists ask their clients to keep a pen and paper next to their bed and to be careful to immediately write all the details of the dream on waking.

For me personally, except for a story I will share below, my favorite time in the sleep and dream cycle is to waken quietly, preferably without an alarm clock, and to allow myself the stillness of the next few minutes to receive whatever messages my mind is sending me. It is a time of passivity, of not initiating any thoughts, of holding on to the quiet and stillness and just absorbing. That is how I first encountered the zucchini message.

Many mornings the message I was awakening to was *How*

are my zucchinis doing?

Have they been invaded yet? Did the bacteria I sprayed on the leaves get rid of the larvae? Are the female plants finally appearing after a wave of male-only flowers?

I was waking up and the first picture on my mental screen was some question about the well-being of my zucchinis. I then learned the next lesson of life:

3. If you want to know what is really concerning you down in the depths of your psyche, just listen in the morning and all will be revealed.

Upon reflection I realized my worrying about the zucchinis wasn't really about the zucchinis as much as it was a window into what was really concerning me. I had a need to worry about something that was dependent on me. I needed to nurture, and I did not have as much opportunity to nurture as I used to.

I was blessed with three children, and as much as I may have complained about it, the reality was that as a father, I was concerned for them.

Were they in good physical health? Were they doing well in school? Did they have friends? Were they good friends? How would they mature? What values would they claim for themselves, and would they be the values I identified with, or perhaps, God forbid, the opposite? Would they find good spouses, make a living, be blessed with healthy kids of their own? The list of worries went on and on. But now that they were older, events were unfolding in real time and on their terms, not mine. The only time I nurtured was when they called with some question or request, and those came rarely.

At the same time, my congregation had continued to grow and prosper. We were widely recognized for the excellence of our synagogue, for the programs and services we offered, and for the quality of our youth activities. I was still very busy, but our staff had expanded to help me, and the uncertainties that both terrified and stimulated me to be more involved and more nurturing were waning.

Even the congregation was growing up and needed me less!

My need to nurture was still very strong, but the needs of many of the recipients were significantly diminished. The solution was to nurture the garden in general, and specifically my poor zucchinis.

With that insight and self-awareness, I never dreamed about zucchinis again. I did, though, have one more very important dream.

Chapter 7

It Came to Me One Night

I have always been fascinated with the creative process. How does an idea, a melody, a picture, or a joke, arrive in the creative mind? I have listened to interviews with some of our greatest Broadway composers who talk of their collaborations with their lyricist partners. Every team has their own method, and sometimes different methods, for coming up with songs for a play. Sometimes they begin with a poem, or even a word, and the melody is then written. Sometimes one line of music comes to the composer and from that they fabricate a song. Lin-Manuel Miranda, when asked on the Rachel Ray television show how he writes songs, said that one song in *Hamilton* took him over a year to get right, and another came to him while on a subway train to Brooklyn. By the time he returned home, it was done.

Many novelists talk about staring at a blank piece of paper with just the vaguest idea of a story, and suddenly characters and plot ideas come to them. The writer Barbara Kingsolver, in an interview with the Daily Beast, discussed her system for writing[2]:

---

2   "Barbara Kingsolver: How I Write" The Daily Beast, Dec 5th 2012.

I tend to wake up very early. Too early. Four o'clock is standard. My morning begins with trying not to get up before the sun rises. But when I do, it's because my head is too full of words, and I just need to get to my desk and start dumping them into a file. I always wake with sentences pouring into my head. So getting to my desk every day feels like a long emergency. It's a funny thing: people often ask how I discipline myself to write. I can't begin to understand the question. For me, the discipline is turning off the computer and leaving my desk to do something else.

I am most amazed by those who describe a process by which the characters they invented take on a life of their own, and as they write the dialogue, they have a feeling the character is telling them what to say.

In my forty years as a congregational rabbi, I conservatively estimate that I have delivered over thirty-five hundred talks and have written many articles.

Some sermons were crafted in a very mechanical way: I had a question that came from scripture or from life. I sat down and researched the issue and wrote a response to the question in the form of a sermon. For some sermons I found the material relatively easily and wrote the sermon immediately, but for others it was painstaking research that led to the answer.

The sermons were usually well received, but to me they were just fulfilling an obligation. There was a slot scheduled in the service for the sermon, and I had to fill it. But sometimes a sermon just came to me. It was as if it wrote itself.

I would start with an idea, and the rest of the sermon seemed to flow from some invisible spring. It felt more like I was recording the sermon than writing it. These were my favorite sermons and the ones I delivered most effectively. They didn't come from my brain but from some place deep inside me, or perhaps outside me, that went directly into my brain and then onto paper. These sermons wrote themselves, and inspired me, and I couldn't wait to share them with the congregation.

One of my favorite sermons that just arrived was about traditions, and no holiday elicits more personal traditions and memories in Jewish people than Passover, and especially the seder. This festive and ritually intensive dinner celebrating the exodus from Egypt is almost universally observed by North American Jews, even when most other practices have been discarded.

This particular sermon was built around the image of the seder table and everyone's assigned seat at the table. My grandfather was at the head of the table with my grandmother, my parents, uncles, and aunts descending from the head of the table in some age-appropriate way and ending with the grandchildren at the end of the table, or worse, at the children's table.

As the years passed, I couldn't help noticing the upward mobility at play as one generation succeeded the next. My father replaced my grandfather, and I was now at the middle of the table. Eventually I was heading the table, smiling at the proliferation of our family and the new crop of kids sitting at the end, or worse, at the children's table.

That image of continuity, of one generation both succeeding the previous and creating the next generation, was a very graphic depiction of the existence of the past, present, and future of our people. That sermon wrote itself and touched everyone in the sanctuary that day.

My usual sermons were analogous to a batter in baseball who regularly hit singles, got safely on base, and kept his batting average at an acceptable level, but the sermons that came to me were home runs. They were out of the park, tape-measure smashes that moved me and thrilled the congregation.

Where did they come from?

I believe the answer lies in dreams, but how?

Dreams have been studied in psychology and in metaphysics.

Michael J. Breus is a clinical psychologist and both a diplomat of the American Board of Sleep Medicine and a fellow of the American Academy of Sleep Medicine. In an article in *Psychology Today*,[3] he summarized the current thinking of psychologists on what dreams are. He lists six totally different and discrete explanations:

1. A component and form of memory processing, aiding in the consolidation of learning and short-term memory to long-term memory storage.
2. An extension of waking consciousness, reflecting the experiences of waking life.
3. A means by which the mind works through difficult, complicated, unsettling thoughts, emotions, and experiences, to achieve psychological and emotional balance.
4. The brain responding to biochemical changes and electrical impulses that occur during sleep.
5. A form of consciousness that unites past, present, and future in processing information from the first two, and preparing for the third.
6. A protective act by the brain to prepare itself to face threats, dangers, and challenges.

---

3   Michael J. Breus, "Why do we dream? New insights into what really goes on when we drift into sleep," Psychology Today, last modified February 13, 2015.

When there are so many different options in the scientific world, the one thing we can be sure of is that psychology has no answer to how creative ideas come to us.

Perhaps the metaphysical world has a better understanding.

Moses Maimonides was a twelfth century rabbi, philosopher, and the court physician to Saladin. Through him flowed the worlds of science, astronomy, medicine, philosophy, metaphysics, and rabbinic scholarship. In his great philosophical work, *The Guide for the Perplexed*, he talks about dreams:

> *Part of the functions of the imaginative faculty is, as you well know, to retain impressions by the senses, to combine them, and chiefly to form images. The principal and highest function is performed when the senses are at rest and pause in their action, for then it receives, to some extent, divine inspiration in the measure as it is predisposed for this influence. This is the nature of those dreams which prove true.*[4]

To Maimonides, the "imaginative faculty" is the receptor in our creative brain that is primed for all kinds of outside influences that arrive in the form of dreams or just arrive in the conscious mind that is at rest but prepared to receive.

On a tour in Edinburgh, Scotland, I was told that one of Edinburgh's most famous sons, Robert Louis Stevenson, wrote a book that would prove to be not only famous and popular but radically different in tone from his other adventure stories like *Treasure Island* and *Kidnapped*. He penned *The Strange Case of Dr. Jekyll and Mr. Hyde*.

---

4   Moses Maimonides. *The Guide for the Perplexed*. Translated by Michael Friedländer (1956): 225.

It is said to be based on a real-life character, William Brodie. By day a wealthy and successful businessman, a deacon on the town council who hobnobbed with the elite of proper society, and by night a thieving, heavy gambling, carousing, sinister lowlife, with at least two mistresses and numerous illegitimate children. In the end he was found out and eventually hanged on the new city gallows he himself had helped to design.

According to this version, Stevenson's creative inspiration for Jekyll and Hyde was the real-life dichotomy of this notorious human being. But I prefer a different, though not mutually exclusive version of how this story came to Stevenson. Stevenson said that often his tales came to him in the form of dreams.

His wife shared that in the small hours one morning, she was awakened by cries of horror from Louis. Thinking that he'd had a nightmare, she woke him, and he said angrily: "Why did you wake me? I was dreaming a fine bogey tale."

That was the origin of Dr. Jekyll and Mr. Hyde.

As I mentioned in the previous chapter, the Kabbalists account for new ideas coming to us in our dreams from the journey each night of some of our souls traveling in the supernal world. They then return with all kinds of nuggets that filter through to us in our dreams.

I know that many people will think this idea absurd and will reject it out of hand. Indeed, a classic Yiddish joke that tells of the interaction of a husband and wife over a dream speaks to this rejection:

The wife sweetly says, "Darling, I had a wonderful dream last night. In my dream you bought me a mink coat."

Her husband has a quick reply: "In your next dream, wear it well!"

But I know of one very personal example of how a dream led to the birth of new creativity and you, my readers are now benefiting from that experience.

I was pleasantly dreaming away at home in my bed, when suddenly I was jarred from my sleep with a powerful sense that something important had happened in my dream. This was not like other dreams that faded within seconds of consciousness. I truly felt something profound had just happened, and I was compelled to record it.

Not entirely awake, but not dreaming either, I quietly snuck out of the bedroom so as not to disturb my wife and hurried over to my study. I turned the lights on and grabbed a pen and something to write on, which turned out to be a small pad of paper. Refusing to fully wake up and lose the dream, I started to scribble away with idea after idea. Each thought was written on one piece of paper, then torn off, and a new thought was quickly written on the next page. I was aware the memories would fade and at a rate directly proportionate to how much consciousness I allowed to return to me. Finally, when all that could be recorded had been written down, I quietly snuck back into my bedroom and returned to sleep.

When the alarm went off in the morning, I awoke with a vague sense that something special had happened that night. But I wasn't sure if it really happened, or if I'd just dreamed it happened.

With the arrival of more and more clarity, I walked over to my study, not sure I would find anything there, and if I did, it wouldn't be any more than scribbled gibberish. Imagine my shock—and ultimately my joy—when I began to read these scraps of paper and realized I had written some profound and fascinating ideas about my garden and life. I immediately knew what I had in front of me was an outline of a book about what my garden could teach me and others about life.

Since this occurred in the years of my rabbinate's greatest

demand on me, I took all the scraps and put them into a folder that would one day be a book. The folder sat in a revered and permanent place in my home study, reminding me that someday I would put it all together and turn this gift from a dream into a book that might help us make some sense of this life through the agency of my garden.

Over the next years while gardening, I would observe interactions between creatures and my garden, between people and my garden, and between me the gardener and my garden, and all these observations were reduced to questions and occasionally answers. Each time this happened, I would leave the garden, enter my study, write down the question or the observation, and then throw it into the file. I was not yet ready to write, but the book was growing.

Creativity may come to us from many different places, but for me, this book was born in a dream.

Chapter 8

Nothing is Forever

Why is my golf game relatively okay for a few weeks and then, unexpectedly, it turns horrible the next week? Why do professional athletes go into slumps? Why does the graph of the Dow Jones look like a rollercoaster and not a straight line upward? Why do we nod our heads in recognition when someone says "Fortunes made and fortunes lost"?

Impermanence is the norm, not the exception. Great landmasses of today were once entirely under water. Glaciers I saw years ago and assumed would always be here are melting before my eyes and may disappear entirely in my lifetime. I am sure the Romans, at their peak, thought their empire would last forever, just as many Americans believe it is their destiny to lead the world forever. We live as though we are the exception and can avoid the one true axiom of life:

4. Nothing is forever.

About two thousand years ago, the poet in Psalm 49 wrote:

Men think that their houses will stand forever,
When they name their estates after themselves.
Man survives not the splendor he cherishes;
His end is like that of the beast that perishes.
Such is the fate of them that are foolishly
complacent,
And of their followers that laud their ways.

My backyard has two kinds of plants. The vegetables are transients. I plant them knowing full well they will last one growing season at most and will then be uprooted to allow for a fresh planting of something else in their spot. (The glory of South Florida gardening is having two growing seasons.) The fruit trees are entirely different. They will be here for a very long time, and while they may not last forever, they should still be standing when I take my leave of this world. Or so I used to think.

Shortly after settling into what was then my new congregation, and long before I even thought of a garden, I knew I wanted fruit trees, especially citrus trees. To a Canadian boy from the land of snow and ice, nothing said Florida like an orange tree and freshly made orange juice.

Of course, I knew nothing about planting or caring for citrus, but the advantage of having a big congregation was there were congregants whose collective knowledge covered everything one could possibly need. A lovely gentleman who had already begun to be an ersatz grandfather to my young children turned out to be an experienced planter of fruit trees. He even had his own secret recipe that included fish heads placed around the root ball of the tree. Under his tutelage we planted a Valencia orange tree and a pink grapefruit tree. We also planted an avocado tree because making great guacamole was a spiritual calling. In a few years, the trees had taken off, growing well and yielding wonderfully. Is there anything better than collecting a bunch of oranges in a bucket today and squeezing them tomorrow into a glass of fresh juice?

Each year the trees grew, and the yield continued to grow—so much so that on a tour of Israel, I found an industrial-type juicer that could handle the volume of oranges I was producing. That may have been the harbinger of the disaster that was around the corner.

In the year 2000, in a failed attempt to stop the spread of citrus canker in Dade, Broward, and Palm Beach counties to protect the nine-billion-dollar citrus industry farther north, and based on what proved to be false science, the state of Florida passed a law that allowed the government to come onto your property and remove all citrus trees if an infected tree was found within nineteen hundred feet.

I received notice by mail that such a tree was found in my neighborhood, and though my trees were perfectly healthy, the state would come by to cut the trees down.

I had watched these trees grow from saplings. I had nurtured and cultivated them and enjoyed the bounty they provided and assumed they would always be there. I used to think that if I ever moved, it would be my trees I would miss the most. For a while we heard nothing from the "canker police." I was lulled into a false calm and hope that maybe my "kids" would be spared.

One lovely afternoon while lying on a lounge in the backyard, I heard a voice coming from the other side of the property. I was startled at first. Who would be coming unannounced into my fenced-in backyard?

I dismissed my first thought that it was burglars, as these voices were too loud, and then I saw them, the soldiers of doom, armed to the nines with chainsaws. With barely an acknowledgment of my presence, they went straight for the tree, cutting into its girth, letting wood chips fly willy-nilly, and before I could fully respond, the orange tree was lying on the ground next to its remaining stump. A few minutes later, the grapefruit tree was history. Only the avocado tree was left standing.

These trees were a large part of my children's upbringing. They participated in the planting, and I would take them by the hand to see and smell the blossoms and later pick the fruit. Now these same trees were lying dead on the ground.

I grieved the loss for a few weeks, and then the authorities returned, again unannounced, to grind the stumps into oblivion. It was like watching a violent death and then having to attend the funeral.

Those empty spaces in the ground and in the air above, where their canopies had reached upward, bothered me every time I went outside. I decided the best response to this indignity, and to the failed permanence these trees represented, was to plant new trees in the same area.

I planted a lychee tree that promptly died. Clearly the killing fields were not ready for new tenants.

At least I had my avocado tree. Now this was permanence. This was power and majesty and it would certainly be here after me.

I had to keep trimming it to keep it at forty feet. It was a Monroe avocado, sadly for the world not cultivated for retail production. Grown to maturity, each fruit had the mass of a bowling ball. The green was full of flavor and the yellow was creamy as butter. For a while my social popularity grew dramatically. I was invited to more parties than ever before, and always at the very end of the invitation, "Would you bring some guacamole made from your tree?"

Now this was a tree for the ages, and the ages it would last!

And then Hurricane Wilma struck. It too liked the majesty of the tree, and especially the canopy, because that is what launched the tree.

Imagine an open umbrella in a windstorm where the wind catches the umbrella from below and starts to pull you up. When the storm was over, and it was safe to venture outside, I saw the crime scene. Strewn about were some thirty avocados not yet ripe enough to eat, and in the middle of it all was the felled tree, running from my backyard onto the fence and hanging over onto the street. Lying on its side, the shallow roots were exposed as well as a layer of the grass that had been uprooted with it. The third and final original tree was now gone. Whether by a human hand or by nature, the lesson was loud and clear: Nothing is forever.

Chapter 9

Counting Means You Count

Whether it is part of the grand plan of a merciful creator or merely the result of the evolutionary process in nature, there is great wisdom to be gleaned in the garden.

After the destruction of my avocado tree and the requisite mourning period had ended, I decided to plant a new avocado tree. I would plant a larger tree than usual, because I wasn't getting any younger, and of course, it would be a Monroe. Surely it would only be a matter of a few years before I would again have guacamole to offer. In the meantime, when word got out I was "between trees," my invitations to parties tanked. I was forced to realize how precarious my social standing really was.

I planted and waited a year, and much to my disappointment, the tree had barely grown. Another year passed and again there was little growth, not only of branches and leaves but also the basic stem, which remained skinny and seemingly malnourished. A horizontal branch did grow, but that was all. By year three I had had enough, and my social life was as sickly as the tree. There was only one thing left to do: plant a new and even bigger tree near the sickly one and see what would happen.

A year later the new tree had doubled in size and was dwarfing the old tree, but for the horizontal branch that had tripled in length and had turned upward. It was considerably taller than the main stem. On a whim I decapitated the original stem and allowed the branch to now become the tree.

The following year both trees flowered and bore fruit. The big, majestic tree had about three avocados, but the little one had more than ten.

I have developed a ritual during the season of the avocado flowering. I wait with great anticipation for the emerging of the buds. For weeks they tease me in their tight clusters as they offer hope for a rich future, but nothing happens. Every few days I go out, waiting to see if anything has developed. It is like a husband whose wife is in her ninth month, full of promise for new life, but nothing is happening. The woman's husband is full of anticipation but helpless to accelerate the process. It is one of the few times in adult life when time seems to slow down and not accelerate. Then the wife announces increased contractions, and he knows the child will arrive soon. The same phenomenon happens in the garden.

After a few weeks of seeing the buds and nothing happening, the first of the buds protrudes, sending out multiple shoots that will host many flowers. They are accompanied by beautiful new red leaves sent like ministering angels to protect these new flowers and the hopeful baby avocados that will emerge.

At this point a triumphant smile emerges, and I enter step two of my ritual. Every day I go out and revel in the increasing amounts of flowers, seeing each one as a potential new fruit. There are thousands, to be sure, and while I know many will never be successfully pollinated, simple logic tells me the more flowers, the greater the likelihood for a bumper crop. Then I begin step three.

I am now on a laser-focused hunt for the first green bumps that will emerge from the flowers. With each one I raise a fist to the sky in a triumphant gesture. I walk from one section of the tree to the next, looking to see which area has mature flowers that might soon yield a small green orb or sadly dry out, turn brown, and fall to the ground, their mission in this drama of life ending in failure.

I am now reflecting on the many—or the few—numbers of emerging fetal avocados and project a joyous harvest or a disappointing season. Even if there are plenty of little green balls, I know the tree will drop many of them. It does not possess the strength or resources to bring them all to term, so I am at peace with those that begin to fall to the ground.

In short order the little pea-sized fruits begin to grow. By the time they get to the size of a large olive, I enter the fourth and most significant part of the ritual.

I count them.

Each day I go out and scan and count. In a good year, the number will still grow, as different parts of the tree will flower at different times. I not only remember the count, but also their general location.

I know there are some at eye level and some even below on a low-hanging branch. Some will be a foot or two above my head, and others will take a while to grow large enough that I will be able to see them dangling from near the top of the tree.

Sometimes I can't find one that I knew was there, but its disappearance is just an illusion caused by the sheltering of the many leaves nearby. Finding them can be as difficult as finding my golf ball after I hit it into the deep rough, and it is sitting at the bottom of the taller grass. Many times, the ball is invisible to me when I approach from one direction, and then it appears when I turn and come back from the opposite direction.

In a great year, the tree will start to shed fruit the size of a small egg, and yet each time I count, the number of avocados on the tree will be nearly the same or even greater because of new ones that emerge.

This ritual will become most important when the crop ranges from medium to small, because the value of each avocado is greater when the numbers are less. From this I learned a great lesson:

5. Things count more when you count them.

If I know that there are many avocados, and the next day a number may have fallen, to me, that day nothing happened, because there are still many avocados on the tree. If I know there are thirty avocados on the tree, and the next day, I count only twenty-nine, I know that one is missing. Where is it? Did it fall off, or did a squirrel in the tree gnaw away at it? Are the others in danger? Do I have to worry about a predator? Is the tree receiving enough water? Is it time to fertilize or spray with copper?

The level of my care is dependent on noticing a change in the tree's census, and I only know that something is missing if it was already counted and accounted for.

One year there was a remarkably small crop, and when the avocados were about three-quarters done, I went out and counted and saw that one was missing. I searched the ground below looking for it, to determine the cause. (I have even been known to perform an autopsy on a suspicious fallen fruit.)

I couldn't find it anywhere, but I did realize that the lawn man had been there earlier in the day to cut the grass. I called him about it, and after asking his men, one worker confessed to taking the avocado, thinking no one would miss it. He obviously did not know he was taking an avocado that counted and would be missed.

Loren Eiseley tells a story of an old man walking down the beach at dawn:

> *He noticed a young woman picking up a starfish and flinging it into the sea.*
>
> *"Why are you doing this?" the man asked the youth.*
>
> *The youth replied, "The stranded starfish will die if left under the morning sun."*
>
> *"But the beach goes on for miles and there are millions of starfish," countered the old man, "so why bother?"*
>
> *The young woman looked at the starfish in her hand and threw it to the safety of the waves.*
>
> *"It makes a difference to this one," she responded.*[5]

Be they starfish or avocados, things count more when you count them.

---

5   Adapted from Loren Eiseley, "The Star Thrower," *The Unexpected Universe* (Harcourt, Brace and World: 1969).

Chapter 10

Never Put All Your Eggs

into One Basket

My avocado trees, unlike my pomegranate tree, have only one season when they produce all the flowers that will ultimately become fruit.

Our human eyes see this annual cycle of flowering, pollinating, growing, and finally harvesting the fruit as the ultimate purpose of these trees.

Nature, on the other hand, sees this little dance differently. To nature this isn't about manufacturing fruit, it is about propagating the species. It is a biological imperative that all living creatures need to produce a next generation. In the animal kingdom, reproduction creates a new generation that will become mobile, and at a certain point in time, leave the birth family and the immediate area of its early days, and move to a different space. There it will continue with its prime imperative to reproduce and propagate its DNA. Plants, on the other hand, are not ambulatory, but nature's imperative is still in operation.

My avocado trees are not related to the trees in *The Lord of The Rings*. They can't suddenly get up and walk down to a neighbor's prime piece of lakefront property, where a permanent source of water is waiting for all their hydration needs. They also can't afford to be surrounded by a dense concentration of next generations that fall from the tree and sprout inches or feet away. So what do they do?

They surround their seed with delicious food that animals (including human animals) will want to take away and eat. Along the way they will eat the fruit and leave the pits behind. Some of those pits will settle into an area suitable for future growth. They will sprout, send out roots, anchor into the soil, and grow into another avocado tree. The fruit is the vehicle that allows the stationary tree to propagate in new and distant areas. The successful growth of new fruit, and its attractiveness to ambulatory creatures, is the key to the tree fulfilling its biological function. In this we see the fruit trees' key for success, but less obvious is another skill that is nature's true genius and the lesson we all need to learn:

6. Never put all your eggs into one basket.

From a macro view, my avocados have only one shot at getting it right. The flowers only arrive in one season with a limited time of blooming. Conditions need to be favorable for successful pollination. Bees must be available to come and pollinate. Winds cannot be too strong, lest they keep the bees away or knock off the flowers or the newly emerging little fruits. Heavy rains and, even worse, violent thunderstorms will interrupt the entire process. All these variables happen in South Florida in late February and March, when my trees are flowering.

I observe the difficulties my trees are facing when in my "ritual." I see the swaying branches and the shedding flowers caused by a few days of strong winds. I watch with great anticipation the emergence of a bumper crop of flowers only to see it followed by two days of continual rain.

In the early learning days, I just assumed that these adverse conditions would lead to a very small harvest of fruit. It was frustrating and humbling to realize how subservient we are to the elements. In our era of so much scientific advancement, we have come to expect that there is a solution to every problem. Daily breakthroughs in science are almost as frequent as breaking news has become on the news channels. And then the reality of the omnipotence of nature enters the scene, and a lesson of humility in the face of nature sets in. But that was not the end of the learning cycle, because I had not yet learned that nature understood all of this and had developed a response.

It was in the micro view that nature showed me how it understood timing and had developed a plan. The tree had the ability to stagger the process. Not all the buds came out at the same time. The flowering varied in both timing and position on the tree. If today five hundred flowers opened and were wiped out by weather conditions, tomorrow five hundred other flowers would open for the first time, and they would be in another area of the tree.

If today's flowers opened and bees were not able to arrive, that section would ultimately have fewer fruits, but the next day a whole different area would have attractive flowers, and if that day the bees were out in great numbers, they would diligently be visiting one flower after the other, successfully pollinating that area. The trees instinctively knew what so many people seem to forget: *Never put all your eggs into one basket.*

Financial advisers always talk about diversification. That is really a fancy word for not putting all your eggs into one basket. Don't put all your money into the stock market. Don't put all your stock market money into one stock or one category of stocks. Why do advisers remind us of this repeatedly? Because people continue to do it all the time.

I remember a congregant of mine who had been successful in making a living, but to provide a lot more for his family, he speculated on the market. When the market was going up, he looked very smart. It seemed, for a while, there was nothing that wouldn't go up, so he poured more and more into the market, until the laws of economic gravity inevitably appeared, and he lost most of his money. Not the additional money that was going to provide the extras for his family, but money for the basic bills he could not pay. He put all his eggs, and some not yet hatched, into one basket and lost it all.

Perhaps the greatest pain I've ever had to deal with professionally was the loss of a child by a congregant. The only thing that made it worse was when it was an only child. Sitting with the bereaved parent as they made funeral arrangements, planning and delivering a eulogy, facing the overflowing crowd of mourners at the funeral all crying and all looking for an answer to why, when no such answer existed, challenged my belief in God, and even more shattered my false sense of security that my children and I were somehow safe from the vagaries of life.

My father was one of seven children, but in reality, he was one of the seven children who lived into adulthood. He lost one brother who died as a child. With the advance of medical science, we take childbirth as a given safe activity for mother and child. It wasn't that long ago that no one took it for granted. We assume, and usually are justified in our assumption, that our children will grow up and survive us. While truer than ever before in our history, some of us will lose a child. Some are not blessed with an option and are grateful for the one child they have, but for many of us, as crude as this might sound, we should have more than one child just to assure that we will be survived by the next generation.

Whether it is because we want to be perpetuated through them beyond our death so we won't immediately be forgotten or because we hope there will be someone around to take care of us in our old age, having more children hedges our bets and diversifies our options for the future.

This concept of putting everything into one basket has far-reaching consequences in society. I am writing this at a time of great social unrest in the United States. The alt-right, and especially the white supremacists, want to return to a vision they believe represents an earlier and better America. An America where all power and control were in the hands of white, male, Anglo-Saxon Protestants. An America where all its eggs were the same and put into one collective basket.

They are so afraid of a diversified America that has left them behind that they hold on to a self-destructive fantasy of racial and religious superiority. They want to live in a world that, pun intended, is viewed in black and white, and they are willing to turn their back on the HD-colored universe we have come to enjoy.

There is no greater example of the danger of putting all your eggs in one basket than this distorted perspective. After all, it was diversity of population that allowed for the cross-fertilization of ideas that propelled the US to leadership in so many fields of endeavor.

How many of these neo-Nazis and white supremacists were delivered by Jewish or African American doctors? How many of them take medicines discovered by immigrants of all colors, faiths, and creeds? How many of the cars (or pickup trucks) that they drive, or cell phones that they use, or software that runs most of their computers and appliances, were invented or built by Jews, Asians, African Americans, Indians, Pakistanis, or other members of the rainbow collection of this world? In truth, who wants to live in their self-contained and sterile world where all of one kind of egg is stored in the basket?

What does it say about us as a species, when my avocado trees are smarter than many of us?

Never put all your eggs into one basket.

Chapter 11

The Art of Survival

When you initially plant a seedling in the ground, it often goes into shock. It withers and droops, and your thoughts immediately go to the dark side.

What did I do wrong? The plant is dying.

Sometimes I did do something wrong. I planted in the heat of the day, in total sunshine and ninety degrees of Florida heat, and it was too much for the seedling to take. Fortunately, most of the time, the plant's shutdown is a defense mechanism protecting its moisture from the elements while it puts its energy into allowing the roots to take hold.

Similarly, when I sow a row of seeds and too many plants emerge, I must thin out the plants to allow space for the others to grow. I pull out some very healthy-looking seedlings, even though it hurts to throw them away.

I sometimes think that my soul must have lived through the Great Depression—or maybe it was just my mother, who did live through the Depression and told me I had to finish my plate because some children in India were starving, that left me with

50

an aversion to waste. So I look for some open space somewhere else in the garden to transplant the seedlings, and the same death or faux death occurs.

Upon reflection, I realize that all of this is the plants' way of surviving, because if reproducing the next generation is nature's prime imperative, staying alive to do so is the ultimate challenge.

Similarly, if I visit the growing garden during the heat of the day, I observe the same drooping of the plants. I realize they are hot and preserving their moisture, so I make sure that on those hot days I water more regularly. There is no immediate response, and I fear that all is lost, yet the next morning when I get up, and before I leave for services, I go out to check on them and there they are, the same drooping plants now standing upright, tall and majestic. I marvel at their ability to survive the heat, preserve their fluids, and then absorb as much water as they can, and through the alchemy of the night, restore their turgor. It is as if they go to bed exhausted and wake up for reveille standing at attention.

The lesson I take from this is:

7. When faced with overwhelming adversity, preserve your assets, conserve your energy, survive, and wait for a more propitious time to come back even stronger than before.

I experienced the human version of this lesson firsthand in my youth.

I was born in 1950 in Toronto, Canada, and lived downtown with or near my grandparents and extended family. Six years later we moved out to the suburbs. By rights, the language all around me should have been English, yet many of my friends who were born in Toronto spoke Yiddish as their first language.

I understood Yiddish since it was the language my mother and grandmother spoke to keep secrets from the children, which meant I was absolutely going to understand and not let on. Even then, knowledge was power.

It was years later, as I learned about World War II and the holocaust, that I realized why so many households spoke Yiddish, and why some of my friends' parents had numbers tattooed on their arms. My neighborhood had a high percentage of holocaust survivors. As we got older and the survivors either healed, or more likely developed scabs to cover the horrors, we started to hear their stories.

They had lost everything. They lost family, possessions, security, and in some cases a belief in God and humanity, but they did not lose the imperative to live.

They did whatever it took to make it through a day, and then the next day, with a drive to survive and tell the world about what had happened to them. In most cases their survival was not random but a result of inner strength to not give in or give up. They followed the prime directive of surviving and then had children whose very existence was an act of defiance against the Nazi monsters.

An Ultra-Orthodox woman in Israel who survived had over a hundred descendants before she died, and each and every one was her response to Hitler and his desire to end the Jewish people.

They understood the message my garden taught me of how to preserve assets to survive and ultimately flourish again. *When faced with overwhelming adversity, preserve your assets, conserve your energy, survive, and wait for a more propitious time to come back even stronger than before.* May their descendants' lives be their ultimate reward.

Chapter 12

Survival Sometimes Means Being Ready to Go to War

No one likes war. Even when it seems necessary or justified from your perspective, someone on the other side has their own reasons for doing what they do. War diverts necessary energy, focus, resources, and time. War leaves casualties and death. If nothing else, the wars of my post–World War II lifetime have taught me that all wars come with unintended consequences. Did anyone see the invasion of Iraq and the killing of Saddam Hussein leading to civil war in Iraq and the creation of ISIS? Yet sometimes war is necessary, and to be a gardener is to be in a constant state of war.

Even in my very suburban home, there are predators who want to consume my "babies." There are squirrels who seemingly have one purpose in life, and that is to eat my avocados. There are birds who love strawberries but insist on eating them on the penultimate day of their reaching perfection, otherwise known as the day before harvest. There are moths and butterflies who spend all their time laying eggs on my leafy vegetables, and especially my defenseless tomatoes, at a rate so fast it seems like I'm watching time-lapse photography. These eggs then turn into little grubs whose entire purpose is to turn into large caterpillars, and who owe all their growth energy to the leaves and fruit of my tomato plants.

To be fair, I didn't start by going to DEFCON 1. I had a long talk with the squirrels and offered them a number of entire avocados in exchange for their consuming a whole avocado rather than sampling a few bites of one before moving on to the second or third. Each sampling was enough to weaken the fruit and make it fall off, often before it was fully ripe and edible. I thought using diplomacy was a wiser way than going to war, so I left the higher hanging fruit alone for them. They responded by inviting a few more members of their family to join them in this itinerant feast.

Game on!

Squirrels are not like other predators for whom this is just a matter of survival. Other predators need to eat, and you are offering them a supermarket of fresh delicacies in their backyard, but squirrels want to take your food and humiliate you in the process. They have a devilish personality. If they could, they would steal your food and do a war dance on your chest. If they had real fingers, they would leave you with a flick of their tail and then turn and flash you their middle finger.

When they refused my rather generous offer of appeasement, I felt it was time to show them my Canadian origins. I left a hockey stick outside with which to chase them, and if possible, practice my slap shot technique. Unfortunately, they are much faster than I am in the ten-yard dash, and they can run up a tree in a flash or fly from the tree to a bush or the rooftop in seeming defiance of gravity.

In the beginning I had the element of surprise. They didn't really know what I was capable of, and I had already shown my weakness by offering a unilateral truce. I could approach them and get quite close before winding back with my stick and letting go with a blow. The fact that I could only get close but never make contact was enough to establish my credentials as a dangerous, if inept adversary. As soon as they heard the screen door shut, they knew I was in the arena, and they assumed their tactical observation and escape plan mode. They did not flee right away, as that would deprive them of the chance to show their complete contempt for me. Rather they assumed a safe space near or on a tree and dared me to attack. If I didn't move, they didn't move, but if I broke into a rush, they were gone in a flash to the top of the tree and then waited to see my next move. If I left, they stayed for lunch. If I lunged forward, they were off like a drone flying over my backyard.

I thought I was unique with my squirrel problem, until one day my wife called me in to see a TV commercial for one of the wireless companies. In it a man was chasing a squirrel all around his pool deck, but to no avail, and adding insult to injury, the squirrel appeared to be laughing at him.

I have tried everything legal to deal with them, and failed. I even bought a special product that promised to emit an ultra-high-frequency noise that would be inaudible to humans but especially unpleasant to squirrels and other predatory creatures. Squirrels are nuisances of such magnitude that the wheel that determined the exact frequency had a special notch just for them.

For a few days, I thought I had won. The squirrels were rarely present, and no new avocados had been gnawed on. Then out of nowhere, I saw the tell-tale sign of their presence: An avocado nibbled around on the outside was lying on the ground.

They had returned.

Maybe the device was too far away from the tree, I thought. I moved it closer, put it on a wheelbarrow, and made sure it was pointed directly at the bottom of the tree where the newly fallen avocado lay. The next day I looked out the window, and there was a squirrel feasting on the fruit while the machine whistled away.

I quietly went outside, careful to not let the screen door slam shut, and videoed the machine with its red indicator light on, proving it was working. I then panned across from the machine to the squirrel who was feverishly eating away. Besides the sick humor displayed in that video, I was secretly hoping the manufacturer would challenge me when I asked for my money back, just so I could send him the video.

War is hell. Losing the war is painful. Being humiliated is the worst of all.

Chapter 13

Never Ignore

Your Enemies

If negotiations with a "higher" animal didn't work, I could at least ignore some of the lower-end nuisances like spiders. After all, besides accidentally walking into a web—never pleasant, by the way—what harm could they do?

> **8. Never ignore your enemies, or one day they may take over.**

My main garden is screened in because of iguanas, creatures so problematic and so frightening that they will receive a chapter all to themselves. The screen has a wooden frame, courtesy of my son-in-law who designed and built it, and it has bird wire for walls and ceiling. Choosing the size of the wire was serendipitous. We chose it for deep and sound reasons—it was all they had— but it proved a gift in that the openings in the wire were large enough to let bees in to pollinate, but small enough to keep many of the moths and butterflies from getting in. It came in a roll that made it clear we would need to attach it to the posts in strips and then overlay one strip with the previous one and attach them with fasteners. This was easy with the walls, but the ceiling required bringing a ladder into the garden and then attaching the bird wire from the right side to the bird wire from the left side.

For a year or two there were no issues, but after a time I noticed there were spiders and webs on the side of the walls, and especially above on the ceiling, both where the side met the top and in the middle, where the right and left side met and were fastened together. I would flick occasionally at a web, but ignored most of it, especially overhead in the middle where I would have needed the ladder to properly reach the top.

I am somewhat vertically challenged and historically lazy, so I didn't bring out the ladder. Why bother, especially since none of this affected any of the plants, including the tomatoes, which often grew taller than me.

Then all my ignoring struck back.

The spiders built their webs through and around the union of the right and left wire strips, putting pressure on the middle of the ceiling. I was oblivious to the ceiling but did notice a dramatic increase in the bugs eating away at the plants. I couldn't figure it out. Finally I looked up, and in astonishment I saw space between the two strips. The ceiling had come apart in the middle from the pull of all the webs, and was all but announcing to the winged insects that the garden was open for business.

In a moment of crisis, it is amazing how quickly laziness disappears. I trekked to the garage, brought the ladder into the garden, stood in a contorted manner looking up, and tied the fasteners all over again, but with two strips that no longer fit easily together, and a major infestation churning away in the garden, I was too late.

Don't ignore your enemies. As my mom used to say, "An ounce of prevention is worth a pound of cure."

Chapter 14

The Organic War

on Insects

Imade the decision early on in my gardening life to have an organic garden. I reasoned if I was going to go to the effort of growing some of my own food, it might as well be not only tastier, but safer than what I was purchasing in the store. When the fence was built, I believed my crops were safe from the birds, iguanas, squirrels, opossums, and God only knows what other creatures existed in my neighborhood. But nothing was going to keep the bugs out.

It is not that I didn't try. I read about how growing some herbs next to some vegetables and some plants next to the garden kept insects away. I'm sure it works somewhere, but not in the Plotkin world. I tried organic sprays on the crops, but they were as effective as the pairing of herbs and flowers with the vegetables.

I talked earlier about zucchinis. I always wanted to grow

zucchinis. Perhaps it's because when I was first introduced to gardens up north, even gardeners with black thumbs grew bushels of zucchinis. Also, zucchinis are such a versatile vegetable and can be turned into everything from soups to breads or noodles. Maybe it was simply because I like eating them.

So from my earliest years in the garden, I have tried to grow zucchinis and I have failed miserably. It is always the same culprit that does me in. There is a bug that attacks the zucchini at every stage of its development.

Long before you see the zucchini flowers appear, there is the growth of the leaves. Initially they are quite big, and to me, rather beautiful, as they establish the food factory for the plant. The stems that hold the leaves push out even farther, and they give rise to the next stage of development: the emergence of male and female flowers. This stage has an intense sexuality that will end in the pregnancy of the female flower.

After conception, there is a fetal growth emerging from the female plant until a rather obvious zucchini fruit is all but ready to be cut from its umbilical cord and emerge full-grown.

That is how it is supposed to be. But it rarely happens in my garden.

The bug invasion begins with the development of the leaves themselves. As soon as they reach some undisclosed size, they are deemed fair game for an attack. At first one notices nothing awry, as the invaders are stealthy in both the timing of their invasion and the location of their deposit.

An egg is never laid on the upside of a leaf, where it would immediately be noticed and discarded before it can cause serious harm. Rather the egg is always laid on the underside of the leaf, where it can hatch and begin to consume the leaf. If left unattended, the larvae will weaken the entire plant and make it incapable of carrying fruit.

In the early years of the garden, I developed a system of following the symptoms to discover the problem. I learned to spot the development of the larvae before they were hatched or, if too late, I trailed the path of their destruction until I discovered them. In tomatoes they would arrive later in the cycle and often went undetected by me until I noticed parts of the tomato fruits were eaten away. That was a sign of their presence, though they remained totally camouflaged to me. I would search for what were now full-grown caterpillars but could not find them until I realized that all creatures that ate . . . eliminated. It was that discovery that allowed me to know they were still there and to follow the trail of waste until I found the culprit. My grandson would probably call me a "poop inspector."

The larvae in zucchini never got to develop into caterpillars. I either got rid of them early on or the plant was weakened by them and died before they grew large enough.

I tried organic sprays on the leaves but never had much success. I was a little luckier with a spray called BT, which was a bacterium that consumed some of the larvae, but that's when the insidiousness of the invader became clear. Even when I had eliminated the leaf invaders so that the plant could now grow strong and bring on the male and female flowers, the moth was even smarter.

It would lay its eggs where I did not spray, right in the heart of the female flower. Thus, while I was celebrating my victory over the bugs, they were secretly and strategically laying eggs within the female ovary so that when conception occurred, not only did a baby zucchini emerge, but inside it was a growing larva. Halfway through the emergence of the fruit, the green color began to turn yellow, and the vegetable began to wither. I cut out the fruit and autopsied the remains, and much to my shock and horror, inside the pulp of the vegetable was a living larva who thought he had died and gone to zucchini heaven. All he had to do in life was eat all day and get bigger.

To compound the problem, if I had any chance to stay ahead of the invasion, I had to check every plant every day, and if I found any larvae, I disposed of them using a highly organic method: I took my thumb and my forefinger, and applied pressure. Low tech and high success.

Unfortunately, an absence of a few days or a week was all it took to allow for a full-scale invasion that overwhelmed the plant. As dedicated to the garden as I was, there were occasional interferences caused by life, like visiting my grandchildren, or a business trip to New York, but even if these could be temporarily handled with the help of others, I had one religious problem. Every seventh day was the Sabbath, and I don't kill on the Sabbath.

Can you imagine the torture to put in as much time and effort as I have described, and then come home from synagogue after services and walk by and know your babies might be under attack?

Who would not want to at least go outside and check that everything in the garden was all right? How appropriate it was that a day dedicated to reflection on the creation of the world could be celebrated by the joy of at least looking reflectively at all that had grown and changed in the course of a week. The garden truly was the place of partnership between man and Genesis.

But what do you do if, in that moment, you see one of the dreaded predators at work, consuming your defenseless children?

That is how I developed my "You are lucky it is Sabbath" speech and flick. When I saw a creature as I toured the garden on Sabbath, I would gently pick it up with the same fingers that were instruments of death during the week and flick them out of the garden and to safety in the great beyond of my backyard, each time declaring, "It is Sabbath; you are spared. I don't kill on Sabbath."

I am pretty sure the larvae weren't impressed, but I must admit I was. I had a sense of spiritual superiority. I felt myself to be holier by my deed and a true exemplar of what it means to be a good observant Jew. I reveled in my self-control and my piety. I was Mahatma Gandhi, Martin Luther King, Nelson Mandela.

Boy was I wrong!

Chapter 15

The Dark Side of the Garden

The garden doesn't just teach, or allow for meditation on oneself and life. It also reflects. In some real way, it is a magical mirror that when stared into not only reflects your visible outside but also reveals the darkest part of your inner self. These next two chapters are the most revealing and most difficult chapters that I have written. In them I will share with you the other, darker lessons of life that the garden has shown me.

No one likes to expose their weaknesses, their moral failings, their inconsistencies, and maybe their hypocritical behavior, but for a book to teach us about life, we must reveal not only the glowing aspects of our nature but the darker sides as well.

The pioneering psychiatrist Carl Jung developed a concept of this darker side, which he called the shadow, and argued it was found in every human being. He wrote: "Everyone carries a shadow, and the less it is embodied in the individual's conscious life, the blacker and denser it is."[6] Roberts Avens posits that the shadow "may be (in part) one's link to more primitive animal instincts, which are superseded during early childhood by the conscious mind."[7]

To ignore or deny it is to suppress the reality of our personal being and to invite no end of psychological trouble for the individual. To acknowledge it and to integrate it into our being, if only to learn how to control or overwhelm it, is a necessary step in our personal and moral maturation. The problem for many of us is that we are blinded to our own shadow and therefore never quite find the way to integrate it into a healthy balance of who we really are.

Here is a story that illustrates the shadow in all of us, and of one who discovered it in time to change the course of the rest of his life.

In his book, *Descending into Greatness*, Bill Hybels, the senior pastor of Willow Creek Community Church, tells the story of a World War II soldier who was part of the liberation of the Nazi concentration camp at Dachau, Germany. Dachau was one of the death camps where thousands of Jews were exterminated. The man told this story:

> *A buddy and I were assigned to a boxcar. Inside were human corpses stacked in neat rows, exactly like firewood. The Germans, ever meticulous, had planned out the rows, alternating the heads and feet, accommodating the different sizes and shapes*

6   Jung, C.G. "Psychology and Religion: West." In *The Collected Works of C. G. Jung*, Volume 11 (1975): 76.

7   Avens, Roberts. "The image of the Devil in C. G. Jung's Psychology," *Journal of Religion and Health* 16, no. 3(1977): 196–222. https://doi. org/10.1007/BF01533320.

of bodies. Our job was like moving furniture. We would pick up each body—so light—and carry it to a designated area.

Some fellows couldn't do this part. They stood by the barbed wire fences retching. I couldn't believe it the first time we came across a person in the pile still alive! But it was true. Incredibly, some of the corpses weren't corpses. They were human beings. We yelled for doctors, and they went to work on the survivors right away.

I spent two hours in that boxcar; two hours that for me included every known emotion: rage, shame, pity, revulsion. Every negative emotion, I should say. They came in waves . . . all but rage . . . it stayed, fueling our work.

After we had taken the few survivors to a makeshift clinic, we turned our attention to the Nazis: the SS officers in charge of Dachau. Our captain asked for a volunteer to escort a group of a dozen SS officers to the interrogation center, and a guy named Chuck . . . his hand shot right up. Chuck claimed to have worked for Al Capone before the war, and not one of us doubted it.

Well, Chuck grabbed his machine gun and prodded the group of SS prisoners down the trail. They walked ahead of him with their hands locked behind their heads, their elbows sticking out on either side. A few minutes after they disappeared into the trees, we heard the rattling burp of a machine gun and three long bursts of fire.

Soon Chuck came strolling out, smoke still curling from the tip of his weapon. "They all tried to run away," he said with a kind of leer.

It was that day that I felt called by God to become a pastor. First, there was the horror of the corpses in the boxcar: I could not absorb such a scene. I did not even know that such absolute evil existed! But when I saw it, I knew beyond a doubt that I'd spend my life serving whatever opposes evil . . . serving God. Then came the Chuck incident. I had a nauseating fear that the captain might call upon me to escort the next group of SS guards; and even a more dreadful fear that if he did, I might do the same thing that Chuck had done! The beast that was in those guards was also in me. The beast within those guards, the beast within Chuck, the beast was also in me. To say that sin is not serious is naive. You and I have a beast within us. It may only reveal itself under the most dreadful of circumstances, but it is there.[8]

Most of us, thank God, will never be so dramatically confronted with the existence and dark potential of our shadow, but we must be sensitive to other opportunities given to us for self-discovery.

For me, it was in the garden that I learned about my full potentiality for acting out my shadow, and it wasn't pretty.

---

8   Bill Hybels, *Descending into Greatness.* (Zondervan, 1993): 144–145.

Chapter 16

The Night of the Iguana

There are very few things in the world that I truly hate. Not in the sense of hating spinach, but a feeling that everything in my body is filled with an emotional rage, a feeling that at any moment during that hate, I am capable of losing control and doing something awful. Nazis I hate, injustice I hate. Ariel Castro, who imprisoned three girls in his home for ten years, I hate.

And iguanas I hate.

For those not familiar with iguanas, they are reptiles that look like Tyrannosaurus Rexes that were hit with a shrink gun. They may be as small as a foot or as large as five feet, but at no time are they anything other than ugly, ferocious-looking creatures with teeth and a long, whipping tail. They are not native to Florida and have no local predators. They are herbaceous, but given those teeth and their looks, I would never risk putting my hand anywhere near their mouths.

Many people have a deep-rooted fear of snakes. Multiply that by a thousand and that is how I feel about iguanas. Rationally, I

69

can explain my aversion to them.

They feast on the tender young plants of the vegetables I grow. Vegetables that, I have already explained, serve as surrogate children. The iguanas love young broccoli and cauliflower leaves and go crazy over emerging string bean leaves.

I will never forget that Saturday morning as I left for synagogue, passing by the garden on the way out of the backyard, when I paused to enjoy one of the great sights of the garden: the emergence of the string bean plants.

Bean seeds are planted in rows about an inch below the earth. When planted correctly, they will emerge in a straight line, first pushing up what will be the stem and then, like something designed by NASA for the Mars Rover, two leaves emerge on either side of the stem and stretch out into a canopy.

I stood at the end of the row and marveled at the precision. It was like a row of soldiers marching in place in a parade ground. I had an urge to salute them. After all, I'd planted them underground and watered them daily, and somehow they figured out how to grow and push through the weight of the earth, emerge erect, and release the leaf canopy.

Three hours later I returned and was aghast at what I saw. Every single one of them had been beheaded.

That perfect row was now just headless sticks in the ground. What could have caused such wanton butchery of my little soldiers?

I asked around and was met with an unexpected question: Were there iguanas in my area? I had to confess I had seen them sunning from time to time, but except for their ugliness and leaving their waste near my pool, I hadn't given them much thought. From that point on, that was all that I was thinking about.

Over the next few months, I planted a variety of vegetables

and learned quickly what the iguanas liked and what they couldn't care less about.

Except for tomatoes and herbs, they liked everything I liked, and I couldn't afford a twenty-four-hour guard. Was this the end of gardening?

That was what led to the building, ten years ago, of the garden cage enclosure I described above. It also led to the beginning of my dislike of the iguanas. Dislike, but not quite hate. After all, I had developed a détente with them, courtesy of the cage.

Hate would come a few years later.

For the next few years, I planted all their favorite crops inside the enclosure and grew the herbs and other vegetables in which they showed no interest in an open patch elsewhere in the backyard. As time progressed two things happened: The iguanas continued to grow larger and multiply, and the integrity of the enclosure began to diminish. This wasn't just a factor of age and weathering. Rather the iguanas had sent soldiers out on reconnaissance missions. They prodded the perimeter both from the ground and from above, near the wooden support beams that they could easily climb.

Iguanas are great burrowers. They would try to come in under the perimeter boards, or over the top if there was a little opening near the posts. Eventually the bigger ones, and I do mean bigger, would push their armored snouts through the bird wire and gain entry.

This invasion did not happen at once but it was continual. I would go to bed enjoying the development in the garden, and the next day I would see something awry.

A broccoli plant had been diminished. A partially eaten tomato was lying on the ground. Apparently they were not interested in tomato leaves but waited for the fruit itself.

Each discovery of a breach led to a review of the enclosure.

I had to find and repair their new point of entrance. With each invasion the level on the hate meter was rising. This was personal, and the enemy was getting bigger, uglier, scarier, and more aggressive.

I had not yet found one in the cage, but I had seen some sunning in the backyard, and I realized I was living with a herd of prehistoric monsters.

I felt revulsion at their appearance, anger at their behavior and to be honest, a great sense of fear. This was the recipe for my developing full-fledged hate. As TV infomercials often say, "But wait! There is more."

One day I came home, and my eye caught some green movement in the garden. I got closer and saw there was a young, smaller iguana running around inside the enclosure, trying desperately to find the portal through which he had entered. I reached for my trusty True North hockey stick, opened the door to the garden, and jumped in. My heart was racing, my breathing was rapid, and I could taste the adrenaline. I wanted him out, and I wanted to see how he left so I would know what repair would be needed. I also didn't want to be attacked.

Now, in full disclosure, I am pretty much afraid of animals, so standing in a contained area and trying to shoo this creature was ramping me up to near hysteria. It didn't seem to mitigate the situation that he seemed as frightened of me as I was of him. I was screaming at him and darting toward him with the stick, trying to poke-check him. I imagine his running around was probably laughable to others, but for me, this was like chancing on a burglar busy at work in my house. Thankfully he found his escape hatch and left.

We had officially arrived at hate!

I closed the opening and reinforced other similar points in the perimeter, but now the enemy had fully engaged.

This cat and mouse game lasted another two years, with occasional breaches and subsequent loss of crops, until we entered a new level of engagement.

It started in the spring, which I learned was their mating season. Female iguanas lay a batch of eggs. The eggs look like small ping-pong balls. In order to lay them, they need to first build a nest, which they do by digging deep under palm trees, at the base of buildings, or as in my case, underneath the raised deck of my swimming pool. For days I would go out and find random holes in my backyard next to a pile of earth that had been displaced. They have been known to weaken sea walls with their digging.

Every day I would fill in the hole, and later it was dug up again or a new one was started. They were now a threat not only to the garden but to the backyard as well. I had multiple shrunken Godzillas messing up my property. I really hated them.

All this, dear reader, is background to allow you to appreciate what happened next.

Chapter 17

The Blood Fever,
Murder in the Garden

"My Sins I Recall Today" Gen. 41:9

My house faces out to the backyard, which has open space, fruit trees, a swimming pool, and the enclosed garden. Behind the fruit trees, and lining the external fence that leads out to a major road, is a strip of areca palms. They are tall and dense and were initially planted as a noise barrier from the main road. The traffic apparently makes a noise audible only to my wife, for I am immune to it, but the palms mitigate the worst of it. They also have become the jungle home of the iguanas and God only knows what else.

As the iguana problem worsened, I would see them sunning themselves in the backyard, and I would quietly go out, get my hockey stick, and chase them in the hopes of permanently solving the problem.

Iguanas when left alone are second only to tortoises in walking slowly. How difficult would it be for me to make a mad dash to them and . . . ?

Unfortunately, iguanas when not left alone go from zero to sixty faster than my car. I think in a ten-yard dash, they could beat Usain Bolt. They always take off in the direction of the areca jungle and disappear into the palms. Until that one Saturday, when everything changed.

We were coming home from synagogue, and as we always do, we entered the backyard through a door in the rear fence. The garden cage is right there, and then the pool and the rear entrance to the house. There is one other structure attached to the back of the house, which we call a sukkah or a booth, and it is used for the festival of Tabernacles.

The booth has a wooden lattice on top that supports the green covering put on expressly for the holiday. The rest of the year, it is naked to the sky, as it was on that particular Saturday. The iguanas were well into a very active mating season, and I had spent weeks filling in holes and closing nests. I was frustrated and angry, and yes, hateful, and for the first time ever, I saw a rather large iguana perched on the sukkah's lattice, probably surveying the backyard in search of the next potential nest. He saw me but seemed to ignore me, perhaps feeling he was safe sitting as high as he was.

I quietly walked to the other side of the sukkah, not making eye contact, and retrieved my hockey stick.

Nothing, No reaction, no movement at all.

I had never been armed and so close to the actual creature. I went under him and gave him a push. He went into overdrive, flying off the lattice, but now found himself with the pool between him and the safety of the areca jungle, so he did something I had never experienced: He jumped into the pool and lay motionless at the bottom of the deep end.

The details of what ensued are not for family reading, but suffice to say, he was never going to be a problem again. But this is not the end of the story nor why I share it. You see, it was Saturday, Shabbos, the Sabbath, and I don't kill on the Sabbath . . . but clearly, I had.

What happened?

From the moment I picked up the hockey stick until the final blow, I was totally cognizant of the fact that it was the Sabbath, and I shouldn't be doing this. And yet I was.

I was literally out of control.

None of my finely honed beliefs and practices, developed over more than sixty years, seemed to matter, and worse, they could not rein me in. I was like a robot guided by remote control. I was out of myself, or more accurately, I had lost control of my shadow, and it was now running things.

This primal response to a primordial creature managed to overwhelm a belief system that I had spent my life developing, and had you asked me in advance, I would have told you it was impossible. "I don't kill on the Sabbath."

When I came into the house and began to calm down, a combination of disbelief and disgust at my behavior overwhelmed me. I replayed for days what had happened, and each time had a recurring sense I was somehow familiar with this experience. It felt like déjà vu, but I didn't know from where or from when. That sense of out-of-control passion, of being so driven I was aware of my actions and still helpless to act differently was not foreign to me, even though I had never experienced it. And then it came to me.

I had seen it on TV.

There are two fictional film presentations that contain nearly all the wisdom about human behavior in the world. One is the

Godfather series, and the other is the original *Star Trek* series.

I was an original series Trekkie. Later I saw the shows repeatedly and never tired of them, but only two episodes stayed with me for the powerful insights they shed about human beings. One was about Captain Kirk being split into two Kirks, one good and one bad, which I talked about in my first book,[9] and one was about Spock when he was in heat.

In an episode called "Amok Time," Spock suffers from the *pon farr*, the time of the mating. For the few non-*Star Trek* fans, Spock is nothing if not the master of controlling emotions. His life is run by logic, and he takes great pride in his father's Vulcan tradition of controlling or suppressing emotion.

In this episode he begins to act strangely. He stays alone in his quarters, throws objects at the wall, and makes strange noises. Finally he begs the captain to take him back to his home planet. But the ship is on a time-based mission and cannot take the detour to Vulcan, and so Spock's behavior becomes stranger. He disobeys orders and has no memory of doing so. He becomes violent, and he cannot explain his behavior. Finally, he confides that if he does not return home to marry the woman he has been betrothed to since childhood, he will die.

He is like an out-of-control teenager, multiplied by a factor of a hundred. His body is pumping out hormonal overdoses that he is powerless to control. Like salmon who swim upstream to the point of near death in order to spawn, Spock must get home to mate, or he will die.

He explains to his fellow officers that what is happening to him "strips our minds from us; it brings a madness which rips away our veneer of civilization."

He goes on to share with the captain, "I hoped I'd be spared

---

9   Paul Plotkin, *The Lord Is My Shepherd, Why Do I Still Want? Ancient Wisdom For The Modern Soul.* (Eakin Press, 2003): 79.

this, but the ancient drives are too strong. Eventually they catch up to us. We are driven by forces we cannot control."

It is quite shocking to watch this transformation happen to the soberest man in the universe.

Later one of the grande dames of Vulcan comes to officiate at the ceremony. She says, "What thee are about to see comes down from the beginning without change. This is the Vulcan heart, the Vulcan soul. This is our way." And she adds, "He is deep in the blood fever."

I can't find a better way to explain what happened to me that Saturday than to say I was taken over by my shadow through my own ancient blood fever.

All my education, all my civilization, all my religious training and practice were not enough to keep my hate under control. It is not something I'm proud of, but it is a teaching moment, taught to me by my garden:

> **9. Never be so smug, so sure of yourself and your ability to always be in control, because there is a time when all of us can break. Never be too judgmental of others, for there but for the grace of God go I.**

Chapter 18

The House

Eventually Wins

Why is continual success in gardening so hard? How can you grow a crop well with relatively little effort one year, and the next year nothing seems to go right?

For years I have enjoyed great crops of tomatoes. I've grown them from seeds and store-bought seedlings. I've bought hybrids and heirlooms, beefsteaks and cherry tomatoes, and usually with enough bounty to eat plenty of tomatoes and freeze containers of soup. Yet this year as I write this book, nothing seems to be working.

Most plants are afflicted with bug infestations. Leaves are curling or turning yellow or brown, and few or no blossoms are developing into fruit. The one exception was a Russian heirloom plant that produced about seven large tomatoes and was attacked by something large enough to eat parts of three fruits. And I have no idea how it got into the garden.

I'm sure there are many agronomists who will give me detailed scientific reasons for all of this. They will say it is lack of crop rotation, not enough organic material in the soil, an emergence of a particular nasty insect that is out of control, or too much or too little water. They have no shortage of potential reasons. They are like weathermen who always tell you what the weather will be and then have no end of excuses why it didn't happen that way. But that is not how I see the world.

For me, everything is somehow a metaphor for the spiritual or theological way of the world.

When the garden is doing well, it is an ascendancy of good in the garden, and when it struggles, it is because evil is in the ascendant. I would answer the opening question of this chapter, "Why is continual success in gardening so hard?" by simply saying there is more evil in the world than good.

Literally applied, it means that if I discover one larva on a plant, I keep looking, because they are almost never one-offs. Even if I only find one, I can be sure there are a few more in there, just more adept at camouflage and hiding.

10. Blessings rarely come in multiples; curses always seem to.

So why is evil so much more powerful than good? The answer may lie in Las Vegas.

Have you ever visited Las Vegas?

It may be "sin city" and "whatever happens in Vegas stays in Vegas," but there is no doubt it is an impressive city. The strip is made up of one magnificent hotel after another with glowing neon, fountains choreographed to music, outdoor pirate boat adventures, and a roller coaster that takes you through a shrunken New York City.

The hotels inside are lavish and the variety of restaurant choices overwhelming. Yet if you look at the actual cost of things like room rates, they are relatively reasonable for their quality and luxury. There are many all-you-can-eat buffets that serve good quality food and even amenities like parking at the hotels that are, by comparison to any major city, ridiculously cheap.

The reason is rather obvious. Las Vegas doesn't make its money the way other hotels and resorts do. They make their money from people's gambling. If you are willing to spend enough time at the tables, you can receive almost anything you want for free. And why does this model work? Because the house will eventually win.

If you spend enough time at the table, the house will win because the odds are always stacked in their favor. Every bet you put down increases the odds the house will win. And that is how I understand evil in the world. Ironically, that lesson is taught from the Garden located in Eden.

The Jewish mystics taught that when God created the world and put Adam and Eve in the Garden of Eden, the world was in perfect harmony. The amount of good equaled exactly the amount of evil, and everything was held in check by this balance. Then the big change happened.

The one commandment given to Adam and Eve not to eat the fruit of the Tree of Knowledge was violated, and they were thrown out of the Garden. At that point the balance was ruined and there was more evil in the world.

From then on, evil was stronger, and it would take more good to restore the balance. If before the expulsion the score was good: 0 and evil: 0, then after the expulsion the score was good: -1 and evil: +1. Now if someone brought good into the world, the first piece would only bring good back to zero. It would now take two parts of good to bring back balance, and only one part of evil to stay ahead.

If this is too confusing or too out there, let me show you this kind of math in a real, concrete way.

If the stock market is at ten thousand and it loses a thousand points, it has lost 10 percent and stands at nine thousand. If it then bounces back and gains 10 percent, it is now at 9,900. To get back to balance, it needed an increase of about 11.12 percent.

It takes a higher percentage to regain balance.

Rabbi J. B. Soloveitchik once taught, "The power of evil is greater than the power for good. A friend sometimes fails to help you when you need him, but an enemy never misses an opportunity when you are down. A man may forget to compliment you when you deserve it, but an enemy never misses a chance to make fun of you."

Here is a little humor that highlights the point, even if it is a little exaggerated:

> *Seymour Schwartz was a good, deeply religious man. When Seymour passed away, God greeted him at the Pearly Gates.*
>
> *"Hungry, Seymour?" asked God.*
>
> *"I could eat," Seymour replied. So God opened a can of tuna and reached for a chunk of fresh rye bread, and they shared it. While eating this humble meal, Seymour looked down into Hell and saw the inhabitants devouring huge steaks, lobsters, pheasants, pastries, and fine wines. Curious, but deeply trusting, Seymour was quiet.*
>
> *The next day God again invited Seymour to join him for a meal. Again, it was tuna and rye bread. Once again looking down, Seymour could see the denizens of hell enjoying caviar,*

champagne, lamb, truffles and chocolates.

Still Seymour said nothing.

The following day, mealtime arrived, and another can of tuna was opened. Seymour could contain himself no longer. Meekly, he said, "God, I am grateful to be in Heaven with you as a reward for the pious, obedient life I led, but here in Heaven all I get to eat is tuna and a piece of rye bread and in the other place they eat like emperors and kings! Forgive me, O God, but I just don't understand . . ."

God sighed. "Let's be honest, Seymour—for just two people, it doesn't pay to cook."

All the difficulties in the garden are a reminder to me that:

11. The challenge in life is to choose the good path, even though we know it will always be more difficult.

Chapter 19

Everything Needs Context

One of my least favorite parts of gardening is weeding. No matter what I try, whether it is mulching or growing vegetables closer to each other, weeds will appear, and if not dealt with immediately, will rapidly grow and challenge the garden vegetables for space, nutrients, and water.

I constantly wonder why it is that the weeds arrive uninvited and with no "sponsor" but take hold, grow, and flourish. Why are they so much stronger and more aggressive than the plants that I chose and nurtured? Why do my plants seem to grow in slow motion, and weeds grow like a time-lapse video?

I thought perhaps they had some super growth-inducing DNA that gave them an edge over cultivated and desired plants, and I wondered why nature allowed them to exist, let alone be so dominant. I imagined them as predators, living off the resident population. I analogized them to criminals swooping in on good, hardworking citizens and stealing all their possessions and material goods. In short, weeds are the bad guys, and why are they here?

Imagine my shock when a little bit of research showed that everything I imagined about weeds was not only wrong but was, in fact, the opposite of what I imagined.

Weeds aren't weeds because it is their nature to steal and exploit the local hosts. They are weeds because they are plants that grow faster than the plants already in the environment. In fact, some weeds, in a different context, are not weeds at all but are desirable.

In Canada after the snow melted, and the brown grass came back to life and grew a fertilizer-assisted green, it wasn't long until dandelions began to sprout everywhere with their full plant structure in sight and bright yellow plants everywhere.

To me, they were a blight on the beautiful green grass that every suburban household toiled to display to their neighbors. Everyone, that is, who did not live in an Italian neighborhood. There I would see first-generation Italian women leaning over the dandelions not for extermination but for harvest. It turned out dandelions were a great source of food and beverages. Every part of the plant was edible, and some people made a coffee-like drink from the roots. Others made dandelion wine.

If I asked that population about the dandelions, I doubt they would have called them a weed. Rather it was an additional crop they could harvest that came as a bonus on their grass.

12. Everything needs to be judged in context.

Many years ago, when I contemplated becoming a rabbi, I read a popular and humorous novel about a young rabbi. It almost stopped me from applying to seminary. The main character was a young rabbi dealing with his congregation, and especially with most rabbis' nemesis, the board of directors.

If American politics today looks fractious, angry, and

ungovernable, put it on steroids and you'd only begin to see synagogue leadership at work. Often the only unifying aspect of a board of directors is the criticism of their rabbi.

In the novel, the rabbi was working with a twelve-year-old boy with challenges, to prepare him for his bar mitzvah. The boy was exceptionally shy, and it was felt there was no way he would be able to stand in front of his congregation and chant in Hebrew his assigned portion of prophetic scripture, called a haftorah.

The rabbi dedicated himself to teaching and practicing with the young man until he could stand on the stage in the sanctuary and chant his portion perfectly. Then it dawned on the rabbi, the boy was practicing in an artificial environment with no people, no coughing, no noise, etc. The rabbi feared that without desensitizing the young man to distractions, he would freeze in front of a live audience. So he devised a drill to help.

As the young man was chanting, the rabbi moved from place to place in the sanctuary, making noise, coughing, and even throwing objects at the lad, training him to focus on the task at hand and ignore everything else.

At exactly that moment, a prominent member of the board (and a leader of the dump-the-rabbi faction) walked by the locked doors of the sanctuary and stared through the window openings in the door. He saw clearly how the rabbi was taunting this poor shy young man, making fun of his disabilities, and torturing him during the practice. This was the smoking-gun proof of the rabbi's character and moral failings, and the board member couldn't wait to call for a special emergency board meeting to fire the rabbi. *Everything needs to be judged in context.*

Chapter 20

I Am Woman,

Hear Me Roar

Throughout most of Western civilization, men have dominated. Women collected and gathered while men hunted. Men fought in the army, men ruled the land, and men constituted the various legislative bodies that ruled with a clear male-dominant outlook. The "fairer sex," it was argued, was fragile, often deemed to be less intelligent, and in need of male protection and therefore domination.

Historically, religions were just as bad or worse, fixing into dogma and ritual the secondary status of women. To this day Orthodox woman sit separately from men in synagogue, and increasingly among the Ultra-Orthodox, they are separated in public gatherings outside of the worship services.

In many traditional Muslim communities, not only is there complete separation in religious services, but many women wear burqas that cover all of their bodies and most of their faces.

They live in patriarchal societies where men make most of the life decisions.

Catholics still refuse to ordain women as priests, and men make the rules that forbid birth control or abortion. Many Evangelicals preach a fixed delineation of gender roles as being ordained by God and that a woman's role is to bear and raise children and be subservient to her husband, while her husband provides for and protects the family. It is so strange, then, that nature shows us many examples of just the opposite.

In a lion pride, the predominant hunters are the females, not the males. The male lions are busy protecting their turf from other males, and of course, servicing the females, but otherwise they are very much secondary players in the extended life of the pride.

I sometimes analogize them to pimps controlling a stable of "working girls" and spending most of their time and energy fighting off younger, hungrier, and stronger thugs wishing to steal the operation for their own benefit.

Killer whales, elephants, and spotted hyenas are other examples of matriarchal societies.

I first became aware of nature and gender roles in the garden, from my ongoing struggle with zucchinis. Not only was I in a constant state of war with the bug that invaded my plants but zucchinis offered me an additional challenge: Where were the female flowers?

Constant vigilance against the bugs, and a little luck, was sometimes enough to get me through the early growing stage of the plant. It then grows larger, with long stems holding large leaves at the perimeter of the plant while the flowers begin to emerge. Each plant contains male and female flowers and the pollination between the two leads to a zucchini growing out of the female plant. I knew I was under a serious time pressure because the bugs were relentless and would return, but if I could get the plant to pollinate in a bug-free environment, I had a reasonably good chance of harvesting a zucchini. And that was when the next obstacle occurred.

The first wave of flowers were overwhelmingly males. Each day a few more flowers would emerge from the center of the plant and grow larger, and yet all or most were male plants. Eventually a female would appear and start to grow out, but often it was too late, as the bugs had reestablished themselves.

This process was true of similar plants, like cucumbers and melons, that followed the same life cycle and were subject to the same bug. In each case I would wonder why so many males were first to emerge, and then finally a female. Why were there so many males and so few females? The answer came after I read about an entire matriarchal family in nature: the honeybees.

In the heart of the hive resides one female queen, and she rules the hive. She is larger than her male workers and lives seventeen times longer than them. She is the only bee able to reproduce, and the drones that mate with her usually die right away or are expelled from the hive. In short, males are plentiful and dispensable, while females are fewer and crucial for the survival of the species. The zucchinis are matriarchal and know this, the bees know this, and the lions' entire way of living is based on this principle.

How did we miss the lesson for so long?

Another plant in my garden, the eggplant, also produces male and female plants. Here the process is a little different. The male and female plants will appear at similar times and will coexist quite nicely. In the absence of bees, they respond quite well to my pollinating the female by pulling over the male flower and rubbing it into the female flower. Occasionally when there is an abundance of male flowers, I will cut the flower off at its stem and bring it over to several female plants.

What is special to me about the eggplant flower is how powerful the female flower is. I have come to think of the eggplant as the Wonder Woman of my garden. The male flowers are soft and wimpy, easy to handle and bend toward the female. The female, on the other hand, is strong and literally prickly in nature. Around the rim, just below the flower of the female, are short but sharp thorns that make you handle the female with great care and respect, lest you get a thorn in your finger and suffer that annoying pain each time you touch the finger over the next few days.

The plant itself is able to hold up the weight of many large eggplants, and so tough and strong that I like to think of the plant as Diana Prince or Gal Gadot, who, when the moment of need occurs, rise up to any challenge and succeed.

The Bible recognizes all these attributes in the Book of Proverbs, 31:10–31:

> *A woman of valor who can find?*
> *Her worth is far above rubies.*
> *Her husband puts his trust in her,*
> *And nothing shall he lack.*
>
> . . .
>
> *Extol her for the fruit of her hand,*
> *And let her works praise her in the gates.*

Where along the way did we all forget that?

If my garden could rewrite the poem in Proverbs, it would probably say:

13. Guys are a dime a dozen, but a good woman is hard to find.

Chapter 21

Cost Effective and Cost Efficient Are Not Always the Best Value

A man is on Fifth Avenue on a bike. Suddenly he screeches on his brakes, honks his horn, and says to the fellow next to him, "Did you hear that?"

The second fellow says, "What?"

The first man pushes aside the grass, and the second man sees there is a cricket there.

"How did you hear that?"

"Easy. Watch this."

He takes out a quarter and drops it on the sidewalk. Notwithstanding all the noise of the people around, twenty-five people turn around when they hear the sound of the quarter dropping.

"How did they hear it?"
"It's easy. It's all a question of what you are listening for."

The question could just as easily be turned around and asked of me: "What are you gardening for?"

In the history of backyard gardening, there have probably been many answers to that question. In World War II, Americans were encouraged to plant victory gardens to help deal with food shortages and stretch their ration books.

In poverty-stricken rural areas of the world, people grow much of what they need to survive.

For those of us blessed to not live in poverty, and where caloric overconsumption is often our biggest food concern, what is our reason for having a garden?

Some answer that they want to grow organic food that does not need to be shipped. They value freshness and non-genetically modified food, and they want to reduce the carbon footprint of their food.

Some want to contribute toward food sustainability, while others wish to avoid factory farming and overfertilization of the soil, and its subsequent danger to our water purity. Some want something to do in the outdoors during the spring and summer weather.

Some want to raise exotic vegetables not easily obtained in local supermarkets, and still others think it's an economical way to supply the food needs of their family.

All the above are valid reasons to garden, but they are not my reason. In fact, my personal experience is such that none of the above reasons work for me.

I have access to many stores that sell organic and GMO-free produce. For much of the year when I am growing vegetables, most of the produce in my stores comes from Florida, and not that far away. I can play golf all winter and enjoy the outdoors, and thank God I saved during my work years and do not need to garden for economic reasons.

In fact, the one thing my gardening does not do is make my vegetables economical.

If cost efficiency were a part of the equation, I would be banished from gardening.

When I look at the cost of materials just to prepare the garden, then the cost of seedlings and seeds, organic fertilizers and mulch, gas to constantly drive and pick up supplies and, most of all, the cost of water—and leaving out entirely the cost of my labor—I have some of the most expensive red cabbages and cauliflowers imaginable.

On a mediocre year for tomatoes, I may easily have five-dollar tomatoes. So why do I do it?

Because as the credit card commercial teaches us, some things are priceless. And that is how I understand the economics of my garden.

I don't just grow vegetables, I raise peace of mind. I lower stress and nurture my soul. I leave the world of plastic and enter a world of earth and nature. When I am wondering whether the plants need more water, or pruning or weeding, I am not ruminating over the trivialities that were my work life. My life and mood used to be defined by what one of my past presidents, who died at a very young age, used to say: "One 'oh sh—' knocks out nine 'attaboys.'"

When my congregation was at its peak in size, I was serving over four thousand people, many of whom thought they could do my job better than me. The compliments were many but lasted briefly, while the criticisms were few but stayed churning and turning in my gut. It would often take days to allow the comment to be processed and eventually discarded or filed away very deeply. During the process I was often in great distress and could find no relief.

Gardening, on the other hand, gave me things to worry about that were not personal or painful. Gardening challenges were about the survival of others, my vegetables, who needed me. I could focus on their problems, and whether successful or not, those problems were never internalized as a personal failing or existential challenge. That is why I garden: because it focuses and relaxes me.

It's not efficient, but it is very effective.

There is a great story that sums up much of what I experience:

> *An American investment banker was at the pier of a coastal Mexican village when a small boat with just one fisherman docked. Inside the small boat were several large yellowfin tunas. The American complimented the Mexican on the quality of his fish and asked how long it took to catch them.*
>
> *The Mexican replied, "Only a little while."* *The American then asked why he didn't stay out longer and catch more fish. The Mexican said he had enough to support his family's needs.*
>
> *The American then asked, "But what do you do with the rest of your time?"*
>
> *The fisherman replied, "I sleep late, play with my children in the hills and the valleys, go to the Basilica, take a siesta with my wife, Maria, and then sip wine and play the guitar with my amigos."*
>
> *The American scoffed. "I am a Harvard*

MBA, and I can help you. You should spend more time fishing and with the proceeds buy a bigger boat. With the proceeds from the bigger boat you could buy several boats. Eventually you will have a fleet of fishing boats. Instead of selling your catch to a middleman, you could sell directly to the processor, and eventually open your own cannery. You would then control the product, the processing, and the distribution. You then could leave this small fishing village and move to Mexico City, then Los Angeles, and eventually New York City from where you would run your expanding enterprise."

The Mexican fisherman asked, "But how long will this all take?"

The banker replied,"Fifteen to twenty years."

"But then what?" asked the fisherman.

The American laughed and said, "That's the best part. When the time is right, you would announce an IPO and sell your company stock to the public and become very rich. You would make millions."

Then after a moment's pause the banker added, "Then you could retire to a small fishing village where you could sleep late, play with your children in the hills and valleys, go to the Basilica, take a siesta with your wife, Maria, and sip wine, and play the guitar with your amigos." [10]

---

10   Adapted from Heinrich Böll, "Anecdote on Lowering the Work Ethic," translated by Leile Vennewitz (1963), based on *Parallel Lives* by Plutarch.

Chapter 22

Eternal Vigilance

A quote often attributed to Thomas Jefferson is "Eternal vigilance is the price of liberty."

I have rephrased his thought for this book: "Eternal vigilance is the price of tomatoes."

Every fall I have a great feeling while preparing the garden for planting. I put in seeds or seedlings and watch the growing process begin. Tiny seeds become little plants with such extraordinary power they can push up an inch of earth to allow a plant to emerge. The plant opens leaves and almost before my eyes, it starts to grow up and out. I watch as day after day the plant grows larger. Some require staking or tying to a trellis for support. The leaves are green and smooth and look like wings attached to the body of an animal. I smile with pride and dream with anticipation of the flowers that will soon emerge that I hope will be the vegetables of a future salad.

The flowers open and I wait for the magic of pollination to occur. Seeing a tomato flower stiffen and then a small ball emerge, announcing the arrival of a tomato, is a moment of immense joy and pleasure. It's a little like seeing the baby bump emerge in your wife as confirmation that a child is on the way. Unfortunately, in the garden there is something else watching the same process unfold, but with a conflicting agenda.

Insects.

I refuse to put poison on the plants. I want an organic garden and am prepared to harvest a lower yield, if need be, to eat natural food without pesticides, though at times it seems a high price to pay.

The cost of eating delicious, flavorful, heirloom, organic tomatoes, is extreme vigilance. Without exaggeration, the tomato plants require at least a daily visual inspection. A newly laid egg can become a plant-consuming larva in hours. When very young and small, the damage they do is survivable, provided they can be eliminated very early. In a matter of a few days, they can grow rapidly, and the fuel of their growth is the tomato plant. They start in the leaves and work their way toward the fruit. Often they are camouflaged and difficult to spot. Their damage is their calling card.

Leaves are eaten or curled and become weakened or discolored. Given enough days the larvae grow large enough to make their way to growing tomatoes and soon begin feasting on the fruit. Enough of them landing and growing on one plant can so weaken the plant that it will droop and die. Daily vigilance is a necessity, but that is when human nature and our regular life become the problem. If I am fortunate to find nothing negative happening for weeks, the drive to go outside and inspect the plants lessens.

It was okay yesterday and the day before, and the weather is so unappealing. I don't have to go out today.

Tomorrow there is a lunch appointment, or a family in crisis needing attention, a sermon to write or a hospital visit, and a bereavement call to make, and I can't seem to make it to the garden during the short daylight hours that are so common during much of our growing season in the south. Now it is two days that I have not inspected.

Sometimes I have trips to take, and while I can ask someone to water my garden, it is too much to expect a friend to want to or be able to do the bug inspection. It is not unusual to return home after a week and see great damage throughout the garden, and especially to my tomatoes. Knowing the problem, and being able to successfully deal with it, is not always possible.

This problem of complacency and the need for regular vigilance is not limited to my garden. It pervades most of our lives.

As I write this chapter, the world has seen the uplifting moment and the power that comes from people sharing together in an act of humanitarian kindness. Divers from all around the world have saved a soccer team of twelve teenagers and their coach who were trapped in a flooded tunnel in Thailand. The odds were overwhelmingly against a successful rescue, and the danger to the volunteer divers was life-threatening, evident in the death of a Thai ex-Navy SEAL.

In discussing the many dangers and pitfalls of the mission, especially after the success of retrieving the first four boys, the divers mentioned complacency as a major risk. To many this may have come as a surprise. With risks involving adequate oxygen, potential panic by non-swimmers navigating distances entirely submerged in incredibly tight confines, how would complacency even enter the equation? But in fact, it is a very predictable aspect of human behavior.

When we are hyperfocused with adrenaline pumping, we are able to muster maximal concentration, but we cannot maintain that degree of attention indefinitely. After some success we inevitably lessen our guard and our focus, and the opportunity for allowing carelessness or error increases significantly.

One of my activities in retirement is to oversee the kosher supervision of a chain of seven kosher deli restaurants in New York and Florida. To do the job properly, I have a staff of eighteen rabbis that I trained to follow my protocols on a daily inspection of the stores. In the orientation I impress upon them how important their job is, because all those who keep kosher and eat in the stores are relying on them to assure them that they are in compliance with divinely decreed dietary practices. It is a trust that has been placed in our hands.

Just as there are health dangers when food purity has been compromised, there are spiritual dangers when the religious purity of the food is compromised. I warn them that one of the biggest challenges to their performance is complacency.

They are human, and after repeating the inspections for a few months and finding nothing to be concerned about, they cannot help but be less focused. In the first few months, the work and the inventory is new to them. They look at every can and inspect every product for the kosher symbol. But after six months, they will probably just give a cursory look. It is exactly at that moment they will not notice that, while the label appears exactly the same as before, the formulation of the product has changed, and the kosher symbol has been dropped from the label. That is when the kosher contamination will occur.

I read of a security guard who worked at the same job, watching the gate of a chemical plant, for fifteen years. For that entire time, no one had ever tried to break into the plant. The guard watched television, read books and magazines, drank sodas, and walked the grounds. Often he would doze off, passing the long, tedious hours in slumber. He hadn't always been that way.

When he was first hired, he sat alertly at his post, making

his rounds promptly and completely. He spent hours working on ways to improve security at the factory. But that didn't last long. The dull routine of the work and the late hours took their toll. As time passed, the guard's enthusiasm waned. One night while the guard slept, three men broke into the plant and made off with thousands of dollars' worth of valuable chemicals and drugs. In an instant, the guard lost his position because of his inattention when it mattered most.

Marriage can be sweet and satisfying, like biting into one of my great tomatoes, but it can be undermined just as easily by complacency and lack of attention. A relationship needs to be nurtured and tended to, or it can wilt and die on the vine.

There is a classic joke about marriage that speaks to the same problem. A husband complains about his wife: "When she is angry, she becomes historical."

His friend says, "You mean hysterical."

"No, I mean historical. Every time there is a misunderstanding, she remembers the bad things of the last twenty-seven years of marriage and how I neglected her."

Like every good joke, there is more than an ounce of truth in that statement.

The same is true for child-rearing.

The timing or our abilities and interests, our health, and our energy is out of sync with the obligations that our lives and society dictate to us. The best time to be retired is when you are young and full of energy and can travel anywhere and do many adventurous activities. The reality is that most leisure travel is done by seniors whose abilities and physical condition limit their activities.

Parenting is best done by younger, energetic parents who have the interest, energy, and stamina to connect with and keep up with young children and teenagers. Yet most parenting coincides with exactly the time in our life cycle when we are most dedicated to advancing our careers.

Young professionals—and today that often means both parents—are forced to give the proverbial hundred and ten percent to their companies or their practices in order to advance and become successful. Many businesspeople are on planes a few days a week. Others stay at the office well into the evening to finish their work. Many young lawyers in a practice are well compensated right out of law school but are expected to put in eighty-hour weeks. Many young doctors, especially those with specialties, are often completing rounds in the hospital well past family dinner hour. The result of all this workload is often neglect of the children. Not only is there is no eternal vigilance, often there is no personal vigilance at all. Instead, much of the parenting is hired out. There are nannies, housekeepers, day care operators, and after-school programs, all designed to be substitute givers of vigilance. But if delegating vigilance is risky for tomatoes, can you imagine what its danger is to a child?

In my forty years of a successful rabbinate, I was very busy, and some of what I point out is not only not unfamiliar to me, it is a confession of my guilt.

(I was taught that when you point your forefinger at someone else, your thumb always points back at you.)

One thing I was able to do was be home for dinner almost every night. Even though I often went back after dinner to teach or attend a meeting, we established dinner as sacrosanct. There was no television at dinner, and cell phones were in the domain of Dick Tracy, so we actually talked. More importantly, we were blessed with a Sabbath that meant that one day out of the week we had a longer Sabbath dinner to review everyone's week, and we had Saturday afternoon to be together. Was it the level of vigilance I would have liked? Not really, but it gave us the opportunity to be connected more than we would have been had we not had some external force making us connect.

When the TV evangelist Jim Bakker went to prison for financial mismanagement of his PTL empire, he thought he'd lost everything. But prison taught him many lessons about where his priorities should be. One day, Jim's son, Jamie, spent the whole day with him at the prison. Afterward, Jamie hugged Jim and announced, "All I ever wanted is to have you all to myself for one whole day. Today was like a dream come true for me!"

Jamie's words broke Jim's heart. He had never realized that while he was building his empire, he had been neglecting his family.[11]

The lesson of the tomatoes and their need for our vigilance is applicable to our jobs, our families, our relationships and almost everything else that truly matters:

14. Complacency is one of life's greatest challenges.

---

11   Tommy Barnett, with Lela Gilbert. *Dream Again: Miracles happen everday!* (Creation House, 1998): 182–183.

Chapter 23

Surprises, a Good Thing

or a Bad Thing?

If you want a greater insight into what kind of person you are, ask yourself a question: Do you like surprises or do you hate them?

When you walk into a darkened room and the lights go on, and a mass of people yell, "Surprise! Happy birthday," do you smile with joy and appreciation, or do you look for the nearest point of escape?

Are you very regimented and do you need to be on top of everything, or are you open and able to go with the flow? Are you an optimist or a pessimist? Is your glass always half empty or half full?

My unscientific observation of people leads me to think that most people do not like surprises.

A man wrote to *Reader's Digest* with an embarrassing story about his former boss. This gentleman was just stepping out of the shower one evening when his wife called and asked him to run down to the basement and turn off the iron she had accidentally left on. Without bothering to grab a towel or robe, the man headed down to the basement. Just as he reached the bottom stair, the lights came on, and a dozen friends and colleagues jumped out and shouted "Surprise!" The man's wife had planned a surprise party for his fortieth birthday.

Many things that are surprises to us end up being bad.

You might go to sleep at night feeling well and wake up with an ache in your body that doesn't go away. After a few days with the pain not getting any better, or maybe even getting worse, you go to the doctor, and after some tests, he begins the conversation with, "I have some news to share with you." That conversation rarely ends well.

Did you ever receive a call at 5 a.m. that contained good news?

On the other hand, you might go to a wedding party knowing that you will know few people in attendance. You plan on a few drinks, a quick dinner, and an early departure, only to find the charming young single woman sitting next to you is the girl of your dreams.

My wife had been single for sixteen years when we were set up on a blind date. I was a recently divorced rabbi, and she was a non-observant Jewish woman. We had about as much chance of clicking as a lion and a lamb had of making it alive together for a day. Yet here we are, married for over twenty-six years.

I've often asked her why she even accepted the date, given the fact that she is one who does not like surprises, has a naturally pessimistic outlook on life, and enjoys being in total control of her environment. Going out with me was uncharacteristic of her general life orientation, except that, luckily for me, she had one exception: She almost never turned down a blind date.

In this one area, she was guided by the lesson that you must kiss a lot of frogs to find one prince. Ironically the number of frogs was considerable and only reinforced her pessimism in the other parts of her life. Yet here I came, and I turned out to be the biggest surprise of her life. I would like to believe that in this case, the surprise was a good thing.

Carried over to the garden, most surprises are indeed negative. The bugs that show up suddenly, or the blossom rot that puts a quick end to a promising tomato. Leaves that looked oh-so-healthy a few days ago turn yellow or begin to wilt. Plants show signs of iguana attacks in my protective reinforced garden plot. That leads to a perimeter check and the discovery of a breach in the cage. And yet there is one surprise that really is delightful. They are called volunteer plants.

Imagine that you have spent months planning and then implementing your garden layout. You know where the tomatoes will be, where the peppers should do the best, and where vine plants like watermelons will have ample area to spread. You want to make sure the taller plants will not block out the sun for the shorter plants, and you maintain a crop rotation within the garden. Like all great plans, some work, and some are a resounding failure. But during all this planning, you walk by a section of the garden dedicated to one crop or the other, and you spot a recognizable plant growing in an area where you know for sure you did not plant or sow it. This is a volunteer plant.

It may have come from a seed dropped by a bird or a land animal. It may be a seed planted in the garden when a tomato fell or was knocked down by an animal. You may have spread compost that had a seed in it. In any case, you rarely get a gift in this world that is spontaneous and comes with no expectations. It is just a surprise, and if it comes in a season when its kin are having a hard time in the area where you did plant them, it may just be the savior of the crop for that year.

In an article in *Mother Earth News*, Sandra Dark writes:

> *Produce from volunteer plants is often bigger and tastier than are intentionally cultivated crops. After all, the plants have sprouted where they want to grow, as opposed to where you want them. Like wildflowers, unbidden edibles usually appear wherever they'll have the best chance to survive and reproduce.*[12]

I always get a charge when I find a volunteer. It is not that I often get the wonderful results that Sandra Dark is talking about. It is more that I just love getting something for nothing. As I mentioned above, though born in 1950, I have always suspected that my soul must have lived before in the body of someone who experienced the Great Depression. I pursue value, I appreciate a bargain, and I can easily do without. Even though today I can easily afford it, I won't buy it if I feel it is overpriced. This is also about the time my wife begins to reassess whether this surprise of meeting me really was a good thing.

So dear reader, you must decide for yourself: Are surprises a good thing or a bad thing?

---

12   Sandra Dark, "Volunteer Plants: A Garden Bonus," Mother Earth News, published May 1, 1980.

Postscript

I wrote this chapter almost three years ago. In editing and rewriting this manuscript, that much time has elapsed. I cannot say that I have been thrilled by this delay, but something happened that has made me wonder if there wasn't a reason all along. As the chapter explains, this year's garden delivered a volunteer. Right next to the carrots and green beans, a plant began to grow. It did not look like anything I had ever seen before. It grew rapidly and ramrod straight. I had no idea what it was, but it grew and began to develop a round, bulbous flower. While it was totally enclosed, I thought maybe it was an artichoke. I had never seen an artichoke grow, but something about the way the flower was wrapped tight gave me the feeling that it would open, and behold, an artichoke would emerge. It did open, and it wasn't an artichoke. It was clearly familiar, especially as the petals of the flower began to develop and become a bright yellow halo around a darker center. It was a sunflower. It grew and then dried out, leaving fully developed black seeds in the middle. I uprooted the plant but kept the seeds.

As a child, sunflower seeds were a regular snack, a poor man's potato chips. When I visited Israel in 1970, they were a poor country's popcorn. People would go into a movie theater and eat the seeds and spit out the shells. By the end of the movie, the trip to the exit was a crunchfest, as the floors were littered with shells. I decided to try a seed, and for a raw, unroasted seed, it wasn't half bad. But at this stage in my life, potato chips do nicely for my snacks.

Rather than throw the rest of the seeds out (see my comments above about having previously been ensouled in a person during the Depression), I decided to plant a few in a small, empty strip of land between two tomato plants and see if any of them would germinate. Over a month went by, and one day I noticed what I thought were a few weeds growing in the empty land. It was not surprising, since I had been regularly watering the area, but these little seedlings did not look like weeds. A week later they developed into what I had earlier seen as the identified plant growing in my yard. They were the next generation of sunflowers.

I transplanted them into different areas of the garden. As I write, they are doing well, and I look forward to their full growth and their majestic yellow collar, looking up to the sun and following it as it travels the sky from east to west. I see them as a message of hope, because I am writing this three weeks into Russia's invasion of Ukraine, and sunflowers are the national flower of Ukraine.

The unbelievable barbarity of Russia is contrasted with the inspirational defiance of the Ukrainian people who are sacrificing everything for the defense of their country. The liberty that we daily take for granted, the freedom of expression, and the ability to engage in disagreements while respecting each other's right to disagree are what thousands of mothers and fathers and children are dying for every day. Like my volunteer sunflower that popped up out of nowhere, the tenacious spirit of the Ukrainian people has seemingly popped up out of nowhere to hold off the mighty Russian army.

Sunflowers look up to the sky for nourishment and direction; the Ukrainians look up to the sky for faith, inspiration, and determination. Whatever the outcome, like my sunflower that somehow showed up, the Ukrainian people will always show up, and will grow straight and tall, and will look up and one day glow in the presence of the sun, as does their national flower.

I have no idea where my volunteer came from, but it can't be a coincidence that that flower arrived this year in my garden. Are surprises a good thing or a bad thing?

Chapter 24

A Definition of Insanity

There is a new popular definition of insanity: "Doing the same thing over and over again and expecting a different result." By that definition, I wholeheartedly plead guilty. I am insane and my snow peas made me do it.

Snow peas are those delicious flat green pods that you encounter in so many Chinese wok dishes. They add color, taste, and crunch to many an Asian dish. I plant them in the hope that I can grow many, as they tend to be expensive, and I have so many dishes that would be improved by their making an appearance. I also grow them because other than tomatoes, they are the only thing that I grow vertically and trellised. This allows me to use a small amount of land for their full harvest.

Their growth cycle is relatively short, and I can get two and maybe even three plantings into one season. Early on, as I learned how to cultivate them, I was able to get decent harvests from three-foot-high plants that remained green and productive. Once the pods started to arrive, regular harvesting only encouraged more to appear, and I was happy. In subsequent years the growth became more challenging, and the yield diminished. Sometimes the plants turned brown too early in the growth cycle, and that resulted in few or no pods growing before the plant died.

I experimented with moving the trellis to a different spot but was never rewarded with the same returns as I'd had at the beginning. In one particularly bad year, I pulled out the plants when they showed signs of going bad early on, added some new soil and sowed again. One year, in desperation, I sowed three times with lackluster results. That year, when I dismantled the trellis as part of the summer shutdown of the garden, I asked myself why I kept planting the snow peas.

If it didn't work well on two occasions, why did I plant a third time when my first two harvests were failures? Was it a sign of premature insanity?

Then I answered myself.

Subsequent planting was an act of hope, and hope trumped insanity!

If repeated failure was a sign of insanity, than all gardeners would be in deep therapy or institutionalized. Failure is a given in the garden, and in life, and continued attempts to overcome obstacles are not acts of mental illness but rather expressions of determination and hopefulness in the face of challenge.

The gift of hope is that we can believe in success in the face of factual failure. We can hope for a positive outcome despite previous disasters. Hope allows us to regroup, to analyze, to evaluate and then correct what we think we may have done wrong.

Was the trellis in the correct position vis-à-vis the sun? Were there weather challenges at key stages of the early growth? Did the soil contain enough ingredients to sustain a healthy plant? Did I water enough?

In trying again there is a sense of exhilaration and anticipation that this time I will finally succeed. Failure is difficult to live with, but depression and hopelessness are much worse. Failure leads to a sense of helplessness, passivity, and victimization. Actions revitalize hope and give us energy. Starting again, especially after a failure, is an anti-depression pill. Action in the face of helplessness elevates us, raises our spirits, and reenergizes us for the challenge ahead.

Every year in December, when the western world is celebrating the Christmas season, there is always a reference to the miracle of Hanukkah.

The Maccabees, having defeated the Syrian Greeks, recaptured the desecrated temple in Jerusalem and purified and reconsecrated it. They attempted to kindle the menorah, the candelabra that was the eternal flame, but only had enough holy oil to last one day, and it would take eight days to make new holy oil. Then the miracle happened. The oil lasted for eight days until the new oil arrived.

I've always felt people missed the real miracle of Hanukkah. It is not that the oil lasted eight days, but that the people had enough hope they bothered to light the menorah in the first place. Previous experience would have reaffirmed the futility of doing so and guaranteed the failure of the effort.

It is not insanity to try something again and expect a different result. It is the divine spark in humans that makes them believe they can engender a better result.

Chapter 25

Every Action Has an Equal and Opposite Reaction

I am of the age group that had to assimilate rapid technological change while living an already full life. When I first came out of school, I would dictate my sermons on a Dictaphone for my secretary to type on a typewriter. She would then give me the draft and file a copy on carbon paper. I still have those tissue-like paper copies of the early sermons. As time went on, the Dictaphone became a digital recorder, and the copies were made on primitive Xerox photocopiers and years later stored digitally on a computer hard drive.

As these changes progressed in complexity, the intervals between them shrank. Every few years we were forced to upgrade. I remember the dread of opening the intimidating instruction manual, which looked like someone had condensed the entirety of *War and Peace* into a booklet. Then I had to master this new device, using new vocabulary and concepts that had just beamed down from another planet.

One day I opened the box of a new cell phone and was shocked that they had forgotten to pack the manual. That's when I was informed that they don't print new manuals anymore. "It's all online."

In more recent times, I have asked my wife how to do something related to a new program, a new device, or an upgrade on some treasured program that no longer responds to the tried-and-true inputs of the past, and she says, "Look it up on YouTube. They always have a tutorial."

This was how I stumbled on a treasury of guided information on gardening and especially on vegetable and herb gardening. What a pleasant surprise not just to learn about something but to have someone show you what they are talking about. That is when I discovered something wonderful about my favorite herb, basil.

I love basil and will often sow it in a pot rather than the garden. I would get lovely plants in the beginning that I would allow to grow awhile before collecting leaves, hoping that they would last longer. I would pluck the larger outer leaves of a cluster and leave behind the smaller inner ones, believing they would in turn grow larger and continue a renewable harvest. My plants continued to grow taller, if less full, and soon the seed pods would emerge signaling the decline of the plant and the beginning of harvesting the seeds for the next sowing.

My problem was that if I saved enough leaves for pesto, I would invariably have a small number of leaves left for other purposes before the plant would go to seed. In addition, every picture of basil plants that I saw seemed much bushier than mine, with lots of thick, dense growth. I attributed the difference to the picture being the one outstanding plant the seed company used for promotion and selling purposes. Then I discovered the

YouTube videos, and I learned an amazing lesson not just about basil but about the nature of life as well:

15. Our relationships are almost always transactional.

If I want a better yield with bushier plants for longer periods of time, the basil plant needs a longer life span. To accomplish that, I had to prune the plant rather aggressively. In fact, according to the YouTube video, for every section of the stem that I cut off, the plant would come back with double the amount of new growth. As Yaakov Smirnoff, the Russian comedian, used to say, "What a country!"

The basil was teaching me about an important aspect of human activity. We are all interconnected, and if we could only understand what we need from each other, we would all prosper.

To understand one another, we must hear each other, and hearing doesn't always mean with our ears. We are all interconnected, and we respond to each other. We are always receiving feedback, but we don't always register it.

Newton's third law states that for every action there is an equal and opposite reaction. There is always cause and effect. That is the human condition. If I compliment you in the morning, I will elevate your mood, I will make you smile, and you in turn will be nicer to the next person you meet. Conversely, if I yell or curse at you early in the day, you will carry an anger and a hurt, and you are likely to take it out on someone else.

When my wife comes home and says something that elicits a powerful, loud, or angry response from me, her first question is "What happened to you today?"

I will ignore the very real possibility of her comment being the cause of my response and acknowledge that sometimes it really is a reflection of something disturbing that happened to me earlier that day.

The best practical application of this lesson is the pay-it-forward movement. What a perfect incarnation of the philosophy of action and reaction. If something good happened to you, then repay that goodness by causing that goodness to happen to someone else.

Dan Pearce, of *Single Dad Laughing*, wrote, "Parenting is the greatest pay it forward system on earth. We don't owe our parents anything. We owe our children everything. The same was true for our parents. The same will be true for our children."

I had parents, and I have children and grandchildren, but thank you, basil, for showing me the way.

Chapter 26

Some Arguments Are Not Worth Winning

I don't know what it was like in your home growing up, but in mine there was a tendency to reduce ideas and people to simple, preferably one-word titles. It reduced complexity, for sure, but it also limited a person to a fraction of who they were. You were the reliable son, the cuddly daughter, the hard-as-nails daughter, or the soft and sensitive son.

The problem with this practice was that it was hard to break out of the image once you were so labeled. Like any other stereotype, whatever you did that fit the label only reinforced it, and any deviation was dismissed as an aberration or exception that proved the rule.

In my family I was the argumentative one. I would argue over everything, and I had to win. From their perspective, I was a dog chewing on a bone who would not let go until they conceded or, in exhaustion, simply acquiesced.

I was better educated than anyone else in the house, but moreover had a strongly developed personal sense of what was right and what was wrong.

This sense was not limited to moral questions. It could just as likely have been applied to prioritizing an activity or disagreeing on the merits of a movie.

What I most passionately cared about was honesty and fulfilling commitments. If I said I would do something, then it got done, regardless of time, inconvenience, or financial costs. In return, I held everyone else to that same standard.

If my dad promised to take me fishing at the dock and then received an invitation to go on a friend's boat, and so he canceled our date, I was not just hurt. I was outraged.

"You promised! You made a commitment to me. How could you possibly renege? You taught us to be honest and to keep our word. How do you now violate the very value you instilled in us?"

I was not a big fan of hypocrisy and loathed lying even more, and I never went gentle into that good night. So I argued a lot.

Once it was established that I was the argumentative one, it was a short jump to pairing that label with an inevitable conclusion. I would grow up to become a lawyer, because I loved arguing so much.

Talk about adding insult to insult—and I can say that . . . because I am married to a lawyer.

Looking back, I wonder why I was so argumentative. Was it because I was passionate about some things, which I have been all my life? Was it because as a youth and young adult I tended to see the world in mostly black and white terms, with only a dash of gray? Was it because I was innately competitive, which I still am? Was it because in so many ways, I was different from the rest of my family? Or was it some form of insecurity that demanded that I be correct all the time lest I be judged harshly for some form of failure?

There is probably some truth in all those suppositions. Our lives are very much like the large slabs of marble that Michelangelo would carve into magnificent statues like David and Moses. When asked how he could take a block of marble and produce such great works, he explained it wasn't him creating the statues. They were always in the stone; he just removed the extra rubble that was concealing them.

The argumentative nature of my personality was part me and part rubble. Given the chiseling nature of life's experiences, the real sculpture of my persona could only reveal itself much later in life, when the rubble was removed and the marble was polished.

In less artistic terms, my persona became more fully developed when I realized that it was not necessary to win every battle. I finally realized that I didn't have the energy or the strength to continue that trait throughout adulthood. You had to pick your battles. Triage the squabbles and save your energy for the issues that mattered the most. Which explains why I don't have a compost bin in my garden.

In my first marriage, I was always right. I won every argument for almost twenty-three years. That might go a long way to explain why there was not a twenty-fourth year. The divorce was unexpected, very public, and left me feeling quite vulnerable. It was very difficult on me, and I chronicled it in my previous book, *The Lord Is My Shepherd, Why Do I Still Want?*

After two years I remarried, and for over twenty-six years, I have not been right once. It is not that I am less knowledgeable now than before, or that I have ceased entirely to argue. It is just that I married someone who argues for a living.

As good as I am at arguing, I remain an amateur in the

presence of a professional. Law school not only taught her to argue and win, it also taught her how to refrain from giving in. She even plays from a different set of rules that I would argue are missing a few basic ethics. Consequently, I have not been correct or won an argument in all this time. For those who believe in karma, she was sent to balance my karmic score in this world.

After we were married and adjusted to so many radical differences in the way we lived our lives, I proposed that I wanted to start composting so I could give the garden its greatest gift: humus.

Humus is the magic nutrient of a garden and a real boon to the nutrient-deficient soil of South Florida. I suggested having a plastic pail that would remain under the sink and that all peelings, shavings, melon rinds, etc., would be put in the pail. Once a day I would dump them into the composter. It made all the sense in the world to me. It was the greatest form of recycling. It was a way of taking literal garbage out of the kitchen and, by nature's own alchemy, turning it into magic food that would increase the vegetable yield in the garden. That is how I saw it in all its simplicity.

My wife's vision, and therefore her position, was entirely different. I was going to take dirty, stinky organic waste and leave it in a South Florida kitchen where it would smell, attracting flies and the ever-present ants. Why didn't I just invite the cockroaches—and maybe even rats—to a daily feast in our kitchen?

"But—" was all I was able to get out before I heard, "This is never going to happen." Her body language said a lot more. The sheer revulsion she felt for this idea was visceral. Blood would spill—my blood, of course—and even then, this idea would never see the light of day.

The young me, the argumentative me, would have put up

a full factual argument. So many people compost, and their houses are not overrun with critters. It is the environmental way of the future. It would enable the garden to be more productive. We would reduce the amount of garbage humanity was accumulating.

The younger me, the one seasoned in the battlefields of life, would have girded for battle. The more mature me recognized a battle not worth having, and certainly not winnable.

The husband who hated and fought kicking and screaming against the expression "happy wife, happy life" also realized that sometimes there was truth in that statement, and so I raised a white flag, and we do not compost in my home.

16. Some arguments are not worth winning.

Chapter 27

If It Hurts, Stop Doing It

I would have never thought of gardening as a contact sport. I've had my nicks and bruises from years of playing pickup sports. Sliding into third base in a softball league, taking a knee in my quad in a ball hockey game, not to mention untold slashes on the hands and wrists. I tore my gastrocnemius muscle on a tennis court and thirty years later tore it again on a ski slope, but gardening? Here I was sure I was safe.

Until I wasn't.

When I first started the garden in Florida, I had to remove the grass to make way for the plot I was turning into a garden. In South Florida we don't have normal sod like most of the country. Instead, we have industrial strength St. Augustine grass. It has the strength, density, and imperviousness of Superman's cape. Hit it with a shovel, and the shovel bounces back.

To clear the grass, one must bang through a section, then get a shovel underneath it and try to prod up the grass using the shovel as a fulcrum. Sometimes the grass gives, and a little piece comes ajar. Sometimes the shovel does not move, and since the body has been set in motion, the body recoils in futility and even pain.

Since I have cleared two plots and expanded or reshaped both over the years, I have had plenty of experience uprooting the lawn. Oh, and did I mention it is ninety degrees with ninety percent humidity?

In addition, as I am away for most of the summer, I always close the garden and cover it with a four- or six-millimeter plastic covering.

When I leave, none of the earth is left exposed, but as the summer sun and the tropical rains beat down on the plastic, cracks develop and areas are exposed, allowing a whole new crop of weeds to grow in the garden. When I return and peel away the plastic, I have the new challenge of uprooting dense, two-foot-high sections of weeds. They are only slightly easier to uproot than the grass, because they at least offer a handle, thanks to their height, and are not packed as densely.

Removing the grass has literally sent me to my orthopedist with a wrist injury requiring an injection. Pulling the weeds has given me frequent back pain, near sunstroke and dehydration.

If this annual ritual of torture was not enough, as soon as the plots are denuded of all foreign matter, they need to be refortified with bags and bags of new soil, organic material, and fertilizer. That means loading the car trunk with large and heavy bags, unloading it, and hauling each bag from the front driveway to the backyard.

It was getting to the point I was dreading the beginning of the season. How many more years could I enjoy gardening before older age would render me physically unable to perform? What was the point of retiring from work with all the time to devote to hobbies, if the body was going to fail me? Then a voice went off in my head. Pain and discomfort were not badges of valor.

17. If it hurts, stop doing it!

You can hire people to do it for you.

Many gardening stores will deliver the heavy bags and leave them at the side of your garden. Gardeners or landscapers, for a fee, will open the garden for you. There comes a time for all of us when we must recognize that we physically can't do what we did before. The cost in pain, injury, or discomfort is too great. So we have three choices:

Continue as in the past while accumulating more injuries and pain until we begin to hate what we love.

Cease doing the activities we love.

Hire someone to do the hardest physical part of the job and leave to ourselves the less demanding but infinitely more satisfying parts of gardening: the planting, cultivating, harvesting, and finally eating the fruit of our labor.

If it hurts, give it over to someone else so that you can still stay in the game.

Chapter 28

The Early Bird Doesn't Always Catch the Worm

I am a go-getter. Not a natural one; I was not born that way. Indeed, I was a procrastinator by early inclination, but I chose an occupation that, to succeed, demanded I maximize time and opportunity. And I desperately wanted to succeed. Even more than wanting to succeed, I feared failure.

Success, for me, meant a large, active congregation with many people attending services and even more having life-altering experiences. To accomplish that, I had to learn how to multitask and how to maximize my return on the investments of time.

When I got a cell phone—and originally, it looked as big as Maxwell Smart's shoe—I would save all return calls for the car. That way I could turn the downtime of driving to the hospital or the cemetery into productive time. Anything that helped to advance the agenda of the day's accomplishments was used.

There were days I felt like Lucy Ricardo in her classic scene, working on the assembly line of a chocolate factory. It all works well for her until it starts to back up, and then it is the classic comedic chocolate disaster.

Even though the garden was an escape, and hopefully a stress-reducer, old habits die slowly, if at all. I began to apply the same tools to gardening. Anything to save time or give me an edge so I could accomplish the garden chores early and have more time for work. I know it sounds sick, in the bright glare of hindsight, but it was who I had become.

In my attempt to achieve not one but two full growing seasons and to try to get as much yield as possible, I tried to open the garden early. This way I could give my plants more time in the garden and be able to give them, at least in the beginning, longer days of sunlight to launch their journey through life.

If I could, I would put veggies into the garden in mid-September and not mid-October when many others would start planting. I was gaining an edge on nature. This was a brilliant idea, except for one problem. Mid-September is still prime hurricane season in South Florida, and some of the most destructive storms have hit during that time.

Even if a hurricane misses you and the destructive winds are farther away, the torrential storms bring rain in copious amounts and with a ferocious pounding that can flood the seedlings, drown them, or otherwise so damage them they become vulnerable to fungus and other predators. In short, the rush to plant can lead to a loss of the crops just planted or to raising weak plants that will barely yield. It is more prudent to wait awhile until most of the danger has passed than to play the bad odds for a questionable gain.

18. **Sometimes the early bird does not catch the worm.**

The worm goes on to a long life while the bird remains frustrated and even more hungry.

Chapter 29

Where Are the

Good People?

If you watch cable news a lot, many of the stories on the nightly news that lead off the show can easily give you the impression that the world is filled with miserable or evil people. That is probably why the nightly news show that I watch keeps putting in features that end the broadcast with an uplifting, feel-good story.

It is not that there are only evil people in the world, it is that good news is often boring, and bad news holds your attention like a captive prisoner. No one rubbernecks at the good, courteous drivers passing them on the other side of the median, but everyone stops at the horror-show of a ten-car pileup or a two-car crash on the side of the road.

It is too bad, then, that most people don't garden, because that is where you meet the nicest people who really want to share and help, and where you see some of the greatest sides of the people you already know.

Because of the traveling and vacations that I would take, I could be away for one or two weeks during the height of the growing season. Just because I was on vacation didn't mean that the plants were off as well. They needed water to grow and develop, and I could never figure out an economical way to have an automated drip irrigation system, so to quote the play, *A Streetcar Named Desire*, "I have always depended on the kindness of strangers." Well, not exactly strangers, but people for whom the garden had no direct connection, but they knew it was important to me and therefore important enough for them to volunteer.

They would come regularly to water the garden in my absence. Two dear friends, Vera and Irene, have stepped up to the plate over the years and helped me immeasurably. They were far from the only ones who volunteered, but in both of them I've found accomplices who care about the garden as much as I do.

19. There really are a lot of good people in this world.

Chapter 30

You Are What You Eat

I am not the only one to have a lifelong complicated relationship with food. I think it is true about most of the American population. We not only enjoy eating, we love experimenting. We want to try the newest restaurants, the latest cuisines, and the most innovative forms of food preparation. We are suckers for ways to add even more calories into a meal.

Who came up with fried butter on a stick at the 2017 Iowa State Fair? Then again, where else could they go after having come up with deep fried Oreos, Snickers, and Twinkies? One answer would be fried macaroni and cheese, with bacon bits and sour cream at "only" 1756 calories a portion.

We know we have an obesity problem in the United States, and yet we are world champions at dissociating the problem from the cause.

How many morbidly obese people seriously ask why they are so heavy when "they don't really eat that much?" They blame it on a slow metabolism or cursed genes.

I blame my father for having given me his body, which, had

it only been six inches longer, could have carried my weight in a much more flattering way. I know it must be true, because he always said it of himself.

I don't know if people really say any of the following, but I am sure everyone relates to it. These are some tips that people have offered to help with dieting:

If you drink a diet soda with a candy bar, they will cancel each other out.

Food taken for medicinal purposes does not count. This includes toast, hot chocolate, and Sara Lee chocolate cake.

Snacks consumed at a movie do not count, as they are part of the entertainment.

Finally, there are those who believe that a balanced diet is a piece of chocolate cake in each hand.

We want our cake and our six pack. We have an entitlement, and when we fail, we find excuses rather than take responsibility.

The garden does not let you get away with this form of magical thinking. It is crucial to know what the causes and effects are between nutrients in the soil and the health of the plant. What the plant consumes has direct consequences on how it grows and how it produces.

The proper amount of nitrogen is crucial for a plant to grow and to remain green, which is essential for photosynthesis. Without photosynthesis a plant cannot absorb the sun's energy. Without nitrogen a plant has insufficient amino acids to make proteins, and without proteins the plant will wither and die.

Phosphorus is essential to enable the plant to convert other nutrients into usable building blocks for growth. Phosphorus deficiency means small plants with little or no flowers and a weak root system.

Magnesium is another essential plant nutrient. It too contributes to photosynthesis, and when deficient will lead to pale leaves. Micronutrients including iron, calcium, copper, and zinc all play a role in healthy plant life. Because we know what they do for the plant and which symptoms develop when they are deficient or in abundance, we can feed the plant in accordance with its needs.

Plants have no denial and no self-delusions. They are truly what they eat. We humans could learn a thing or two from plants and the relationship between consumption and health.

20. We, too, are what we eat.

Chapter 31

Mann Tracht
Un Gott Lacht

Prior to college most of my education came from attending parochial school. It was a long school day that covered all the secular requirements as well as Hebrew immersion and Judaic studies. By the time we got to high school, our day got even longer and our subjects even more cumbersome.

I remember in tenth grade taking Hebrew, Latin, French, German, and of course, English in the form of literature and social studies. If that was not enough, I had a passing knowledge of spoken Yiddish just from listening to my mom and my grandmother speak. There were days when I could have three vocabulary tests in three different languages. I could be asked, for example, to write the antonyms for a word in French and my mind would first respond with a Hebrew, Latin, or German answer. One of the lessons I learned that year was the complexity of idioms and the impossibility of translating them literally.

There is a British idiom, "Let sleeping dogs lie." It means "leave well enough alone," or as I saw it described in its twenty-first century version, "if it ain't broke, don't fix it." Imagine if you were told to translate "let sleeping dogs lie" into another language. You would use the word for dog and for sleep, but it would make absolutely no sense. Similarly, an idiom in one language may have a rhyme that is entirely lost in translation. So it is with the title of this chapter.

The Yiddish means, "Man plans and God laughs," but since it rhymes in Yiddish, it is ever so much pithier. The Yiddish captures the pathos and the sad acceptance of life's negative surprises. It is like a fatalistic balm that we put on to deal with all the failed hopes, frustrations, and disappointments that are so ever-present in life, and especially in the garden. If you are going to try to grow vegetables and herbs, then you are strongly advised to learn this lesson and to commit it to heart.

21. Man plans and God laughs.

Gardeners are always advised to plan long before the first shovel enters the ground. You must design the layout to maximize the variety and the yield of the garden. You must know which plants need more sun and which need only partial sun. You can't have the taller plants in front of the shorter ones, or they will block out the sun. You must rotate crops, and you must decide which crops to grow from seed and which from seedlings. You need to know what your consumption needs are so as to not have an excess of one crop and an insufficient amount of another. After you have planned all of this and many more considerations, you must know that some, if not most of what you planned will probably not happen as you hoped.

If you are lucky in the first year and certain crops grow

well and produce in abundance, you naturally assume you will recreate the same result next year. Unfortunately, what works one year does not necessarily reoccur the following year.

The first time I planted strawberries, I had a wonderful experience. The few plants I put into the ground grew well, yielded well, and were off the charts in their sweet and juicy taste. Birds did not get to them before they were ripe, insects ignored them, and the experience of going out early every morning to pick the shiny, ruby-red berries, and eating them right away for breakfast was indescribable. It was great, and I looked forward to having that experience every year. It was also the last time I had that degree of success.

Mann tracht un Gott lacht.

How does one psychologically handle so much disappointment? It is really a simple calculation. Nothing in life is guaranteed, but it is absolutely true that a hundred percent of all crops not planted will never be harvested. Once we understand the realities of garden life, we can move on to practical actions to deal with the problem.

22. Learn to acknowledge defeat.

I have previously discussed the challenges I have had with zucchinis. I had two options, and I've tried them both. The first was to keep trying yearly, or occasionally skipping one year after which the passage of time allowed me to convince myself that I had a new way to solve the problem. And of course I had not solved anything. Or the second option: I could acknowledge defeat, move on, and look for something that would work in the garden.

Why put so much time, effort, hope, and garden space into the zucchinis that would break my heart when I could plant

135

more string beans that seemed to grow beautifully, and with fewer challenges? What about trying something new every year?

It is never good to be on autopilot. We need to hope, to dream, to aspire for some new conquest, some new goal that we have a legitimate shot at attaining.

For years I grew broccoli from seedlings and with considerable success. One year I wondered what it would be like to grow it from seed. Should I sow it directly in the ground, or grow it in a pot and then, at a certain size, plant it in the garden?

One year I saw a nine-pack of cauliflower seedlings, a vegetable I had never grown before. I knew I could grow broccoli, but I wondered if that space could be used for something else like cauliflower. I was rewarded with a bumper crop and a new challenge. What do I do with so many cauliflowers? The problem sent me to cookbooks and recipe websites and new discoveries. I learned that the much-heralded cauliflower pizza was a dud, but cauliflower soup was a gift that I would have never tasted but for the need to use and save the crop.

If you have reasonable expectations in life and then know that no matter what you do, there are aspects of life that you have no control over, you don't give up, but you do move on. Sometimes the only response to the jokers that appear in life is to look up to the sky and say, *"Mann tracht un Gott lacht."*

Chapter 32

The Biorhythm
of the Garden

While it may not be true that there is "no crying in baseball," it is true that there are no days off in gardening. The commitment to gardening is very much like the commitment to child-rearing. It is not that you must be there every day but that if you are away, you need to arrange for coverage.

I always find at the beginning of the gardening season that work and devotion are not hard to muster. In the fall when I begin, I am full of energy and optimism. I can barely wait for the time in each day when I can get out and do what is needed that day. First there are the chores of getting the garden ready. Then comes the planting and watering. But mostly it is the anticipation and joy of seeing the plants take off. It is a lot like seeing my grandchildren after a few months and marveling at how much they've grown since their last visit.

As long as there are signs of growth and development, I am

all in. How can you not get excited when you see the first tomato flowers open, and even more so as they stiffen and reveal the emergence of the "belly bump?" First it is a pea-sized ball, then an olive, then an egg, and finally a full-sized, recognizable tomato.

Next the focus on the tomato changes from size to the changing of color. The green starts to turn yellow, and then the yellow morphs into red. Finally it is time to harvest and eat. It is not hard to stay energized when there is so much positive feedback.

Unfortunately, I don't live in the perfect garden.

Not all the crops follow this successful trajectory. Some give partial returns with lower yields. Some have problems developing and never produce.

In the middle of the season, you can handle the failures with the thrills of the successes, and the great Floridian do-over called a second planting. But then the inevitable biorhythm of the human being takes over. We can sustain concentration and energy for only so long before our enthusiasm wanes and the call for rest or diversion takes over.

This explains vacations. No matter how much we love our jobs, we reach a point where we simply say, "I've had enough. I need a break. I'm due for a change. I have to get away."

My personal biorhythm was established, as I'm sure were many of yours, by spending most of my first twenty-five years on an academic calendar. September meant getting back in gear, focusing on school, developing work habits and a work ethic, and for me at least, dreaming regularly of the end of June and time for vacation at the cottage. By May of each academic year, spring fever was in the air, and it was hard to stay focused on academic accomplishments. In some sense it was helpful that there were final exams, because the fear of taking them and the terror of failing them overcame my psyche's desire to start summer vacation earlier than scheduled.

My gardening biorhythm is no different. It demands a heavy work schedule, but at a certain point, it also wants a vacation. What was a nuisance in November becomes a major pain in April. My behavior reflects this change in attitude. I tend to the garden's needs with less attentiveness. I am physically and mentally exhausted with the garden. I am tired of chasing the bugs and the weeds and the diseases, all of which seem to increase with the arrival of greater heat and humidity. At the same time, the plants themselves present a picture of tiredness and finality.

There are no more new growths or new blossoms. We are in the final stretch. Vegetables do their last growth spurts or their final ripening, and then it is clear that they are finished, and all I can think is, *Great, I'm done. I hate this gardening. I need a break. I want freedom from work and freedom from worrying.*

There is a true sense of relief when the plastic cover goes over the plots.

A magical metamorphosis will eventually happen. There is only so much rest a human being can handle. Come the end of July, I feel an emotional resurrection.

I miss the garden. It seeps into my dreams. I start imagining how I will plant in the coming year. I start sketching a diagram of how the rows will look filled with different plants in a new order. I have reasonable optimism that the crops will be better, and the yield will increase. I have new seeds that I have never used before. I buy seedlings I have never tried, and I can't wait to see how they grow and how they taste.

In the last few years, I have come to enjoy brussels sprouts and have discovered many new ways to prepare them, so I decided to grow them. Frankly, I had no idea how they looked in the garden. The plant emerged looking like it would grow into a cabbage of sorts, but then the plant grew an ever-longer stem with a mop-like green head, which I assumed would contain the sprouts.

The stem kept growing taller and thicker until it was more like a staff, but it had a peculiarity. Bumps started to emerge on the sides of the stem. It looked like it was developing a bad case of acne. I was still waiting for the sprouts to emerge from the top when I realized those pimples were growing into something familiar. They were the brussels sprouts.

As the older ones matured and the younger ones continued to emerge, I started to pull off the now clearly developed sprouts and turned them into a vegetable side dish. Finally, when the season was over and the acne disappeared, I pulled out the stem and had a vision that I was holding Moses's staff. I wondered if I could part a sea with it.

This is the pot of gold at the end of the rainbow that emerges in the joy of the beginning and ends in the successful harvest of something you never grew before. Then you rest, and with joy and optimism, begin all over again. This is the biorhythm of the gardener's life.

23. Life is not linear, it is circular.

Chapter 33

When is a Bargain

Not a Bargain?

Like a lot of people, I enjoy a good bargain. Finding a real bargain is a great feeling. You sense that somehow you scored big. It isn't that you cheated anyone, it's more like you outsmarted someone or something. You waited just long enough for that coveted item to go on sale, and not so long that they were out of your size.

You recognized the intrinsic value of the item when no one else did, and you captured it at a lower price. You are allowed to brag about a bargain. You can flash your mercantile prowess without seeming to be a braggart, and all everyone wants to know is if there are more such deals available for them. And there is no greater bargain than getting something for free, unless you are in the garden.

The garden doesn't demand backbreaking labor, but it does demand its needs in the right amount and at the correct time. Besides nutrients and sunlight, the garden demands adequate watering.

Without a computer-driven drip irrigation system, you have no certain way of knowing if your plants are receiving their needed hydration. Hand-watering is time consuming and physically demanding, so you would think that the greatest gift a gardener can receive is rainwater. It costs you nothing in money, labor, or time. It is the ultimate freebie, the bargain of all bargains. Except you have no control.

Imagine that you have just planted seedlings, or that new seedlings are emerging from seeds planted in the ground, when a tropical wave appears in the atmosphere. For the next two days, you are pummeled with lots of water delivered with great force. The kind of rainstorm that flash floods are made of.

The furrows between rows can fill up rapidly and overflow onto the planting row. The supersaturated soil can begin to erode, leaving the young plants with nothing to hold onto.

Some proud plants standing erect are mashed down, causing them to forever remain as invalids who will grow up deformed and weak. Some leaves will become moldy and cease to cause photosynthesis while passing on their disease to the newer leaves. An entire season can be in jeopardy.

24. Sometimes free is no bargain at all.

Chapter 34

A Few Short Takes

When you buy a seed pack, you receive a bunch of seeds that will become a specific plant. The seeds are not a mixed group. The seed company is selling you pure seeds. When you open the package, they all look the same, and yet after planting, no two plants will grow exactly the same, look exactly the same, or yield the same.

How can that be?

Have you paid attention to your family? You and your siblings all came from the same parents and none of you are the same. Some of you look more alike than others, but no two of you are identical, nor do you follow the same life trajectory or have the exact same personality. That is the reality of nature. We are all related and similar, and yet we are all different.

~

Eyal Shani is a celebrated Israeli chef. In an article in *Tablet Magazine*, he said:

I see myself as a servant of the Almighty, not as a creator. It's a privilege to observe the act of creation, the primal intent of every vegetable. Who is this vegetable, what is it, what does it want, where might it feel pleasure, where might it suffer, what are its aspirations? This is how we fulfill our role as human beings in this world. We are the operators of God's software, whether we do it through cooking or something else. But the moment I try to create something myself, I lose.[13]

That is the transcendental that I find in the garden.

---

13   Liel Leibovitz, "Eyal Shani, Israel's Most Celebrated Chef, Opens New York Restaurant," Tablet Magazine, last updated February 2, 2018, .

Chapter 35

Conspiracy of Silence

There are great conspiracies of silence in life, and perhaps leading the list is aging. There is so much about aging in general that no one ever told me about, and even deeper secrets about aging males.

Women are told about menstruation and menopause. They know about their bodies shifting after childbirth and about wrinkles and changes to the very skin we live in. Men are oblivious and uninformed.

As I have experienced my sixth decade of life, I find more and more changes to my body that I didn't know were coming.

Why didn't I know that aging meant decreased testosterone, which meant that muscle would disappear and be replaced by fat? Why was I not informed that fat was twice as likely to be affected by gravity as muscle?

My dad used to take me to a steam bath, where older people would sit naked in a wet steam room and sweat profusely. When they got up to walk, I noticed a similar body shape between them that appeared to me to be an aberration of nature. They looked like I imagined very pregnant naked women would. In fact—and I will try to explain this gently, so as not to offend—many, it would seem, had not seen their private parts in years, and if they had looked in the mirror, they would have been shocked at how low they now hung.

Why had no one told men that the ever-present libido, which had in many ways guided our every thought and action, would one day take a long vacation without a forwarding address?

When I was a child, I never understood why people would wear those half-sized glass lenses which lay farther down on the nose, such that these people would always be peering over their noses as they looked at you? Had no one ever told them how stupid they looked? Why did I not know that in your forties, your eyes change?

Why didn't I know that those old people with large brown liver spots didn't always have them, but years later they suddenly appeared, uninvited and undesired?

Why did I not know that urological changes would take over and revert urinary pattern and bladder control to the same frequency as infants in diapers?

To this day, when watching television shows geared toward seniors, I learn about medicines and treatments for problems I didn't know were humanly possible, let alone waiting for me in the dark shadows.

That is how I feel about gardening.

I did not come from a family of farmers. My maternal grandfather was a shoemaker, my paternal grandfather a ritual slaughterer of kosher meat and a ritual circumciser. My father was a salesman, and my mother played mahjong. The closest any of my family came to a garden was cutting the lawn. Why did no one tell me how special working with nature and soil could be? Why was I, a developing clergyman, never told about the transcendental nature of the garden?

How come from a young age I knew about hockey and baseball but nothing about growing food? Why did I think that herb was someone's first name?

I had never even seen or heard of an avocado until I was seventeen and went to California to visit a girl who I hoped would at least be a long-distance girlfriend.

(I should be grateful that I had been given a brief, if somewhat detached lesson in the birds and bees. Which, come to think about it, was probably the only nature lesson I ever received.)

Maybe it was because we were an emerging middle-class family with an emphasis on upward mobility tied to success in education, and that working with your hands was seen as something to graduate from, not a direction to return to.

We were raised to pursue professions, white-collar jobs, and to be the bosses, not the bossed.

The joke in my world, growing up, was "Become a doctor. If you can't stand the sight of blood, then become a lawyer, and if you are mentally retarded"—we were not politically correct in the '50s—"be an accountant."

Maybe it was that we were Jewish, and had two millennia of having land taken away from us, that sent us away from the land. What country in Europe did not expel its Jews at some point in its history and then confiscate their land?

I was born five years after World War II, five years after a third of my people were murdered just for being Jews. Five years after my grandmother's large Polish family, including those who worked the land, ceased to have land or life. So the land was not important, because you could not trust being rooted to it. But knowledge, information, and skills were portable. You could take them with you, and no one could confiscate them.

Why would anyone encourage gardening as a pastime?

    Maybe, ultimately, this is why I am writing this book.

    Maybe this is my way to help break the conspiracy of silence.

Chapter 36

String Beans Taught Me to Not Fear Death

As I write this chapter, I am seventy-two years old. I have been retired from my synagogue for six years, and I have enjoyed every minute of retirement. I enjoy complete control of my time, for the first time in my life.

My parents controlled the first stage of my existence, followed by school, career, and family. I got up every day and looked at a to-do list that was generated by everyone else's needs. Only after completing those tasks did I begin to tend to my own needs. I have no complaint for what was, but I offer no excuse for what is now. It is the freedom I dreamed of, and it is now a reality. I also am aware that I need to enjoy every day, because this stage of life won't last forever.

I have daily aches and pains that now arrive without any apparent cause. I tire more easily. I don't hear everything as clearly as I once did. I have glasses for reading and distance, and a special pair for working on the computer. My daily routine begins not with morning prayers but with a slew of pills and vitamins that come out of a container divided into the days of the week. Thank God, most days I know what day it is without having to check a calendar. I remember most things, but the recall time is now minutes or days, not seconds. I could win many a Jeopardy game if they allowed a pause button.

I am much more emotional than in the past, and I tear up easily, not only in movies, but often watching a feel-good story on the news. I reflect on the past. I think of legacy all the time, and I know that regardless of how long this period of life continues (and I am in no hurry to end it) it will end one day, and I will die.

I always assumed that thought would frighten, if not terrify me, but it doesn't.

When I was a young rabbi and called on to perform the funeral of a child or young adult, it was a very difficult and painful task, but it wasn't personal. There was a unique reason to that death. An accident, a birth defect, a weird infection caught on some exotic trip. There was always a way to explain why what happened to them was unique, a one-off, that had nothing to do with me.

When my contemporaries died, there was a family medical history, a reckless act, or an emotional or financial crisis that led to a suicide. There were countless reasons for their deaths, all of which I was magically protected from. My ability to practice cognitive dissonance knew no boundaries. Death existed, but what did it have to do with me?

Lately my denial skills have waned, together with all my other skills. Too many people in the news are dying at near my age or younger. I am no longer the overachieving kid. I am no longer the youngest one in the room—just the opposite. One of my friends and colleagues told me of a recent dinner with a few of his old-time friends that he hadn't seen in a while. During the meal he was shocked at how many times the phrase "of blessed memory" came up in conversation.

I no longer deny that death is a personal reality, whether it comes in a year, a decade, or—if you are listening, God—at least two decades.

Now really is the time for me to fear death.

But I don't.

I wasn't quite sure why until this year, as I was gathering the last string beans of the year. I was shocked to realize that my string beans were comforting me.

I love growing string beans. You put a seed one inch in the ground and several days later something subterranean is pushing up. After breaking through the soil, they quickly emerge erect, unfurl two leaves and daily show demonstrable growth and secondary leaves. Shortly after, they present the first flowers that will become string beans.

Of all the plants in my garden, they are one of the fastest to go from seed to harvest, so they give rapid positive reinforcement. Even better is the fact that the more you harvest the beans, the quicker they are to offer more flowers, and therefore more beans. You can go daily into the garden and pick beans for that day's dinner. After a short break, the new beans arrive again, and the daily picking resumes. Of course, nothing in life is that good, so there is a catch. The quality of the beans diminishes in successive harvests.

The beans in the first two picks are beautiful. Long, slender green beans that detach easily and fully from the bush. They are crispy and tasty, with little to no development of large seeds inside.

With the passage of time, the beans become shorter and

stubbier. They are less tasty and with larger developed seeds. They do not detach easily from the plant, either breaking in two or pulling off the entire branch, leaf and all. The leaves, by now, are turning brown and drying out. In a little while, when picking the last string beans, the entire plant can be uprooted. In short, I have just described an entire life cycle from birth to death, and yet as I was pulling the last stragglers of the crop, I was overwhelmed with a sense of what a great life the plant had had.

During its life it grew strong and accomplished.

It raised many potential progenies. It did what it was created to do. It did it well and lived to see success and to be appreciated. It produced well into old age and finally arrived at the one last point that was always there and inevitable. Its life was never about the destination, but always about the journey.

I identified its journey with mine. I am seventy-two. I too was once young and strong and productive. I had three pulpits over forty years and led the last congregation for thirty-three years. I have received many professional accolades and held interesting leadership positions. I hosted a television show, published a book, served on the law committee of my movement for over two decades, and for me most spectacularly of all, I gave three invocations before Miami Dolphins home games, and had a two out of three victory record.

I was blessed with the opportunity to touch so many people's lives, and to be helpful in times of joy and sorrow. I met many famous and important people and traveled through most of the world.

I am blessed with a wonderful family. I have a loving wife, and my three children are all college graduates, happily married, and have produced seven grandchildren. They are proud practicing Jews, active in their communities and helping others along the way.

I chose to retire when I did not because my congregation wanted me to but because I could see the changes that were happening to me. Like the great string bean plant, my leaves were starting to dry and wither, my produce was not up to the earlier standard, and I didn't want to be the last string bean on the plant that uprooted the entire bush when it was pulled.

I look at my life through the trajectory of the bean plant and realize it has been a great life, and hopefully it will continue in a new way and with a different agenda, but I will eventually be unable to escape the inevitable destination. So why fear it?

My death is preordained. No living creature lives forever. No matter what waits for me in the future, the accomplishments of this life remain and cannot be taken away. It has not been a life wasted. It is a life lived.

As in the garden, the bugs, the diseases, the challenges of weather all came to me but never cut short the life I have been given.

The beans have been harvested and consumed, and the seeds live on in others that have come along, and who knows? Maybe I will see another generation, if I am blessed to see great-grandchildren. So thank you, string beans. You have illuminated the road ahead.

So:

25. Why fear death?

The end.

Epilogue

After I finished this manuscript, two events occurred that were so monumental and potentially transformative of life as we have known it that I feel I need to address them. We were first struck with a worldwide pandemic that had us in lockdown for months, and then the murder of George Floyd and the demonstrations for Black Lives Matter. If, as I have argued, the garden is a source of wisdom and life lessons, then surely there is something to learn from it relating to these two dramatic upheavals to our lives.

One of the questions about the pandemic that was asked of me, as a rabbi, was how could a loving God allow such a plague to attack millions of people in the world?

A young woman who had grown up in my congregation wrote to share her observation that the world was getting scarier and scarier, and that it seemed to her as if we were being sent one plague after another. She felt like this was a replay of the ten-plague story of the Bible.

My best friend forwarded his synagogue's newsletter to me,

and I read his rabbi's column. In addressing this very question, he put the onus for what was happening on people's behavior, and he exhorted his congregants to see this as a call from God for us to pray to Him for forgiveness, and to change our ways to engender divine grace and forgiveness.

I did not know whether I should laugh or cry. When discussing this with my fifteen-year-old grandson (a certified genius, I may add) even he heard the uncomfortable nature of this answer and asked if this wasn't the same question that some people asked of the holocaust.

This is a theology that blames the victims. It is an approach that is guaranteed to seed the next generation of atheists. And who could blame them? I told my grandson that Hitler and not God killed six million Jews, and I told him, and the young woman, that Mother Nature with the help of people, and not God, sent us the COVID-19 virus.

The virus is not a punishment from God but a direct consequence of man's efforts to disrespect nature. We intrude on nature's space with more and bigger cities and introduce animals with unique viruses to other animals, when in the past they would have never been in contact with each other. We eat things that are "exotic" and then bring those microbes into our population, which has no immunity to them. Jews understand that there are limits to what people can and should eat from the animal world if we are not able to exist in God's first choice for us, namely practicing vegetarianism as Adam and Eve did in the Garden of Eden. We can at least keep kosher as a control and a limitation on what is available to us.

We heat the atmosphere and disregard the warnings, and then we reap superstorms and other forms of global weirding.

We produce enough food to feed the overpopulation that we caused and then distribute it so that the haves take most of it and the have-nots receive much less. Every time we do not respect nature and do things because we can—and not because we should—we upset a delicate balance. And it always comes back to bite us.

Pandemics are not God's punishment for us, but rather man's punishment from nature for having abused the planet. Actions have consequences, and if you abuse Mother Nature, she will surely come back and punish you.

The rise of pandemics does not come as a surprise to gardeners. We see manifestations of it every day in the garden. I have written earlier in the book of all the diseases and pests that we encounter in the garden. Our garden is humming along nicely, growing, flowering, and holding out so much optimism for a bumper crop. And then one day, we walk in and leaves are shriveled and yellow, or riddled with holes. We turn the leaves around and see an outbreak of insects munching their way across them. The plants are weakened.

If we aggressively attack the bugs, we may save the crop, but even if we do, it will be lesser in number and quality.

Sometimes it is not a visible critter but a puffy mildew or some other fungus that causes a robust plant to go into seeming cardiac arrest and die, almost without warning. Denying it, thinking it has only hit one plant and will go away, magical thinking, or hoping for a miraculous cure will assure that the crop will be ruined. Only prophylactic actions, attentive treatment, or immediate treatment give us a chance to ward off the worst. It is even more difficult in an organic garden with limited remedies, so action needs to be forceful and immediate, and it doesn't hurt to have a little bit of luck.

There are some other interesting comparisons to the pandemic outbreak that we also see in the garden. How is it that in a row of seven tomato plants, some are overrun, and others seem unaffected by the attack?

Each plant is different, even if it is of the same kind as the other. They all have their own level of immunity. Some are naturally more gifted at warding off the disease, and some may be asymptomatic while being exposed or even infected. Some plants will respond to treatment and others will deteriorate and die no matter what we do.

Gardeners know the attacks are coming and have developed coping mechanisms. We practice social distancing: Often we will plant the same crop in two different and separated areas a few weeks apart. This way if one crop is attacked by a horde of insects who are at the peak of their life cycle, the other crop will grow after most of those pests have ended their lives.

Good gardeners are always attentive. They do not avoid testing because of some misbegotten idea that "what I don't know won't hurt me." Rather they are always testing, always on alert, and ready with a plan. Good gardeners do not run away from experts and scientific data, they seek it out. We have extension offices with help lines and newsletters that tell us what bugs are affecting our area and how to cope with them.

Potatoes grow with their heads in the ground, not gardeners!

As to the protests over Black Lives Matter, what we are really talking about is the acceptance and even the appreciation of diversity. There is an unfortunate need among humans all around the world to go tribal and to differentiate their tribe from everyone else. Especially if their tribe is lower on the economic or social level than most everyone else. They need someone to be lower than them. They will resent those above them and try to scapegoat someone in that group as the reason they have fallen behind. They will revel in their superiority over another group so they can at least feel they are better than the other. What a shame these people do not garden or do not listen to their garden, because we gardeners love diversity.

In the garden, green is the new white, and it is represented by some lettuces, string beans, herbs, and some types of zucchinis. But have you ever seen a garden in full bloom with black eggplants; red, yellow, and purple tomatoes; red, yellow, and orange peppers; red radishes; white cauliflower; and multicolored lettuce mixed? Not only is it visually stunning, but dietitians tell us that multicolored fruits and vegetables contain a lot of antioxidants. Given a choice between eating a regular potato and a blue one, the latter is much more beneficial for you. Similarly, biodiversity is crucial for the survival of our planet, and losing so many species to extinction is a great threat to our existence.

If we could embrace diversity in our society, it would dramatically strengthen our country, maximize the latent talent of all our people, and bring greater prosperity to all of us, while reducing the differences that add nothing but sap all of us of so much of our vitality.

As I write these words, I am forced to come to grips with another reality of the virus. I have lived in South Florida for forty-two years and have never spent an entire summer in the heat and humidity of a Florida summer. The shortest vacation the synagogue ever gave me was a month's reprieve to go to Canada and cool down. This year, the virus has taken that trip away from me. It has also taken away my granddaughter's bat mitzvah celebration, and the opportunity to see and hug all my grandchildren. (My children have learned since the arrival of grandchildren of their own declining status in the family.) All the Zoom meetings in the world cannot compensate for the loss of physical proximity that I feel, and so the garden will have to restore to me some familial equilibrium.

I started gardening to compensate for my need to nurture

when everyone in the family no longer needed my nurturing. I look forward to returning to doing that nurturing now more than ever.

Every day when I look outside and see the garden, I start imagining next year's garden. I review what worked well this year and what I want to do differently. I already have my seeds, which I can start earlier than usual, since I will be here in August. I do not know when I will see the family again, and that saddens me, but imagining the new crop going into the ground gives me a big smile. If life gives you lemons, make lemonade.

To everyone, I raise my glass of lemonade and say "L'chaim."

Life Lessons List

1. Nothing worth doing is going to be easy, especially when it started that way, and even with hard work, the results will never be guaranteed.
2. Think long term, act short term.
3. If you want to know what is really concerning you down in the depths of your psyche, perhaps totally repressed from your conscious mind, just listen in the morning, and all will be revealed.
4. Nothing is forever.
5. Things count more when you count them.
6. Never put all your eggs into one basket.
7. When faced with overwhelming adversity, preserve your assets, conserve your energy, survive, and wait for a more propitious time to come back even stronger than before.
8. Never ignore your enemies, or one day they may take over.

9. Never be so smug, so sure of yourself and your ability to always be in control, because there is a time when all of us can break. Never be too judgmental of others, for there but for the grace of God go I.

10. Blessings rarely come in multiples; curses always seem to.

11. The challenge in life is to choose the good path, even though I know it will always be more difficult.

12. Everything needs to be judged in context.

13. Guys are a dime a dozen, but a good woman is hard to find.

14. Complacency is one of life's greatest challenges.

15. Our relationships are almost always transactional.

16. Some arguments are not worth winning.

17. If it hurts, stop doing it.

18. Sometimes the early bird does not catch the worm.

19. There really are a lot of good people in this world.

20. We, too, are what we eat.

21. Man plans, and God laughs.

22. Learn to acknowledge defeat.

23. Life is not linear, it is circular.

24. Sometimes free is no bargain at all.

25. Why fear death?

A Note from the Author

The only thing better than eating a fresh vegetable from your garden is sharing it with a friend or loved one. If you enjoyed this book, please write a review and post it on your social media accounts, the online store from which you purchased it, or the AIA Publishing website.

Acknowledgments

Writing a book is relatively easy; getting it published is very challenging. The rejections accumulate quickly and challenge your confidence in yourself and in your work. There were many times that I considered giving up on the project, but someone always seemed to come forward with a compliment or strong words of encouragement, so that I was able to cast off the doubts and continue. I want to thank Stella Harvey, whose encouragement and guidance after reading one of the early drafts was manna in the desert. When no agent was willing to take me on, Richard Curtis sent me a contract and loved my work as much as I did. He was water in the desert for a parched wanderer. Finally, my wife, Cheryl Kaplan, listened to me read every chapter after I wrote it, and as I held my breath, she smiled, gave me a thumbs-up and told me it was good, keep going.

I would also like to thank Dr. Vera Joffe and Irene Kivetz Moore, who over the years took care of my garden whenever Cheryl and I were away. Without them, the garden would have failed, and this book would have never happened.

Book Club Questions

1. What did you learn from the book?
2. Did any of the author's experiences or lessons relate to you? If so, which ones?
3. Which of the life lessons were most important to you?
4. Which of the life lessons do you disagree with?
5. If you could talk to the author, what questions would you ask him?
6. Have you ever experienced the need to nurture? If so, what happened when there was no one left who needed you?
7. Did the book make you want to garden?
8. The original title of the book was *The Rabbi's Garden*. Would you have preferred that title or the published one?
9. How do you feel about messages that come to you in a dream?
10. How did you feel about the war with iguanas? Do you see them as hostile enemies or creatures that should be left alone?
11. Who do you most want to read this book?
12. Of all the information presented in the book, what has stayed with you the most?

CPSIA information can be obtained
at www.ICGtesting.com
Printed in the USA
JSHW020522240223
38155JS00001B/1

9 781922 329448